THE BATTLE OF
FRANKLIN

THE BATTLE OF
FRANKLIN

WHEN THE DEVIL HAD FULL POSSESSION OF THE EARTH

JAMES R. KNIGHT
SERIES EDITOR DOUGLAS W. BOSTICK

Charleston   London

THE
History
PRESS

Published by The History Press
Charleston, SC 29403
www.historypress.net

Copyright © 2009 by James R. Knight
All rights reserved

First published 2009
Second printing 2010
Third printing 2010
Fourth printing 2010
Fifth printing 2011
Sixth printing 2011
Seventh printing 2012
Eighth printing 2013
Ninth printing 2014

Manufactured in the United States

ISBN 978.1.59629.745.6

Library of Congress Cataloging-in-Publication Data
Knight, James R., 1945-
The Battle of Franklin : the Devil had full possession of the earth / James R. Knight.
p. cm.
ISBN 978-1-59629-745-6
1. Franklin, Battle of, Franklin, Tenn., 1864. 2. Tennessee--History--Civil War, 1861-1865. I. Title.
E477.52.K58 2009
976.8'63--dc22
2009037685

CONTENTS

ACKNOWLEDGEMENTS

The Civil War is the most researched and written-about event in American history. In this short account of the Battle of Franklin and the events that surrounded it, I'm simply telling a story that I've learned from many other historians who have done a lot of the heavy lifting before me, and I'd like to thank a few of them.

For an overall view and account of the war, it would be hard to improve on Shelby Foote's majestic three-volume work, *The Civil War: A Narrative*, which introduced me to the subject many years ago. James Lee McDonough and Thomas L. Connelly's *Five Tragic Hours* and Wiley Sword's *Embrace an Angry Wind* brought the events of late November 1864 at Spring Hill and Franklin the academic attention they had so long deserved. Most recently, Eric Jacobson's excellent study of Franklin and Hood's Tennessee Campaign, *For Cause & for Country*, has become the gold standard. This would have been impossible without them all.

Finally, I am indebted to the folks at the Carter House Historical Site at Franklin, Tennessee, and its archives. To Thomas Cartwright, the dean of Carter House historians and its former director; and to David Fraley, who holds that position now—thank you. To Alan, Angell, Elizabeth, Bobby, Dennis A. and Dennis P., Jim and all the others who have welcomed an old retired guy and given him a chance to walk the ground and tell the stories to a lot of nice folks, some of whom have come seeking a long-dead relative who fought or died here—thank you. You've all taught me more than you know.

PROLOGUE

The Farmer and the General

Franklin, Tennessee

November 30, 1864

Sunrise

Fountain Branch Carter was worried. Columbia Pike, the macadamized road that ran in front of his house at the south edge of this small town of about eight hundred people, was crowded with Union soldiers and their horses, wagons and artillery pieces, with more stretched out along the pike as far toward the south as he could see. His yard was filling up with men in blue, pitching tents and starting campfires. An officer had knocked on his front door and gotten him out of bed before daylight, and now his parlor was serving as the field headquarters for a Federal division commanded by Brigadier General Jacob Dolson Cox, with staff officers and messengers coming and going in a steady stream.[1]

It wasn't as if Carter had never dealt with Yankees before. The Federal army had controlled this part of middle Tennessee and had a presence in and around Franklin for over two years—even building earthwork emplacements for artillery on the north bank of the Harpeth River, which they called Fort Granger—but this was different. Before, it had been a few thousand men—a few regiments or a brigade or two—but this was a whole army. By lunchtime, well over twenty thousand Federal soldiers would either march past Carter's house or take up residence in the line

Fountain Branch Carter, owner of the Carter House, the Union field headquarters. A sixty-seven-year-old grandfather, Carter led a group of his family and neighbors—half of them children—down to his basement, where they hid as the battle rolled around the house. *Carter House Archives.*

of entrenchments that ran one hundred yards south of his front door. Carter had already taken some precautions in case there should be fighting—he had hidden much of his food, for instance—but now he had some hard decisions to make.

Fount Carter was a sixty-seven-year-old widower and farmer with a large family to consider. Moscow Carter, his oldest son and a paroled Confederate officer, was living with him, as well as four daughters and a widowed daughter-in-law. In addition to the seven adults, there were also nine grandchildren under the age of twelve. His first thought was to move his family down into town, but General Cox offered to let them stay in the house. He explained that as soon as they got their wagon trains across the Harpeth River, the army would be moving on to Nashville. If there was any fighting at Franklin, it was expected to be east or west of town, assuming that the Confederate army would try to outflank the Federal position as they had done the day before. Everyone agreed that a frontal assault on the line just south of Carter's house would be extremely foolish and very unlikely.

Carter and his son Moscow had discussed the general's offer and decided to keep the family together in the house, as much to keep down the pilfering by the soldiers as anything, but they also agreed that everybody should pack a small bag of essentials, just in case they had to run. Both men knew that nothing is certain in war. Things could change very quickly.

In spite of General Cox's assurances, Carter noticed that his men were already working to improve the old earthworks that ran south of his house and stretched around the south edge of the town, anchored on the Harpeth River to the east and west. Even more ominous, there was a Missouri unit digging a fallback line of entrenchments just behind his smokehouse and farm office only twenty yards away, and six artillery pieces were being moved into position in his backyard. Not an encouraging sign. If the mainline gave way, the battle could very quickly be right at his back door.

Oaklawn—Home of Absalom Thompson
Two Miles South of Spring Hill, Tennessee
November 30, 1864
Sunrise

About fourteen miles south of Fountain Branch Carter's front yard, which was rapidly filling up with Federal troops, another man was facing the new day in a foul mood. Only half Carter's age, Lieutenant General John Bell Hood commanded the Confederate Army of Tennessee, and seven of its nine infantry divisions were camped nearby along the Columbia Pike, south and east of the town of Spring Hill. Twelve hours earlier, at sundown, Hood believed that his troops were in the process of taking control of the Columbia Pike and trapping most of the Federal troops who had been delaying him for the last week. Upon waking this morning, however, the general found that the road was never actually blocked and that the entire Federal army, except for some burned-out wagons and a few stragglers, had escaped. At this very moment, in fact, they were streaming past Fount Carter's house and digging entrenchments across his farmland and around his cotton gin. To say that General Hood was unhappy with the turn of events would be an understatement.

Ever since Hood had taken command of the Army of Tennessee four months earlier outside of Atlanta, he had faced criticism and doubters. He had replaced General Joseph E. Johnston, who was loved by the men of the army, and had been promoted to command over other men who the officers of the army would have preferred. Hood didn't have Johnston's experience, patience, maturity or endearing personality. What he did have was a reputation for personal bravery, sacrifice (he had been wounded twice leading his men) and aggressiveness, sometimes to the point of rashness.

Most importantly, Hood also had the support of powerful men in Richmond, including President Jefferson Davis.

Hood soon had several clashes with some of his senior officers, and after Atlanta's fall, his most senior and respected corps commander demanded to be reassigned rather than serve under him any longer. His detractors accused Hood of being strategically grandiose, tactically unimaginative, logistically sloppy and physically unfit—he had a paralyzed arm from Gettysburg and a stump of a leg from Chickamauga. Because of these infirmities, he had to be tied on his horse every morning, and he carried a crutch and wooden leg strapped to his saddle. To be fair, however, even though many have charged that his handling of his troops in the defense of Atlanta resulted in unnecessarily high casualty rates—and they may be right—it's hard to see how he could have prevented the loss of the city.

No one questioned John Bell Hood's personal bravery or his commitment to "the Cause." He had already given more than most. What they questioned was whether he was really the best commander for the last Southern army still able to maneuver and mount any sort of offensive action between the Army of Northern Virginia, now besieged by Grant at Richmond, and the Mississippi River. With this new push into Tennessee, he intended to prove them wrong. He had brought his men across the Tennessee River and meant to threaten Nashville and even move as far as the Ohio River, if possible. The first real resistance had come a couple of days ago at Columbia, and in response, he had planned a grand flanking maneuver worthy of his heroes, Robert E. Lee and Stonewall Jackson. In Hood's mind, the sun should have risen today on a great victory, but it had all come to nothing. The enemy had escaped.

Hood had been on the field the day before, within easy reach of both his subordinates and the battlefield itself, but when things became confused and began to go wrong, his efforts seemed to only add to the confusion. Maybe his damaged body was exhausted from eight days on the road from dawn to dusk; for whatever reason, as the sun was going down, Hood chose to leave the execution of whatever plan he had at Spring Hill to others, and now he felt they had failed him.

As with most failures, at Spring Hill there was enough blame to go around. A more experienced, more mature, more personally secure commander might have simply accepted the blame as the senior officer on the field, as Lee had done after Pickett's Charge on the third day at Gettysburg, and gone forward to correct the deficiencies within his command with as little impact on morale as possible. This Hood could not do.

The Farmer and the General

Rippavilla Plantation, home of Major Nathaniel Cheairs and site of General Hood's breakfast meeting the morning after Spring Hill, November 30, 1864. *Author's photo.*

Hood had called for a breakfast meeting of his senior commanders at Rippavilla, the home of Major Nathaniel Cheairs, which still stands today on the Columbia Pike, just south of Spring Hill. As the general and his staff rode across the fields toward the fine plantation house, he was furious.[2] In Hood's mind, he had been the victim of incompetence if not outright disobedience of orders by some of his corps and division commanders, compounded by what he believed to be the general unwillingness of his troops and their officers to attack fortified positions. In some of this, Hood's feelings were understandable—the performance of some of his subordinates was certainly open to question. Hood's suggestion that the troops and their line officers were too hesitant to attack fortified positions, however, was unjust and unfounded, as many of them would shortly prove with their blood. It was also profoundly insulting to proud officers like Patrick Cleburne and others.

The breakfast meeting that morning was private, which was just as well. Given General Hood's mood, the language would certainly not have been fit for women or children. As far as Hood was concerned, he and his plan had fallen victim to the mistakes of others. What he would later call "the best move in my career as a soldier"[3] had been wasted, and by God, he would know the reason why.

This then was the way Wednesday, November 30, 1864, began for two men. One of these men was a simple farmer and businessman—a father and grandfather responsible for a few of his children, workers and neighbors and caught between two great armies. Other than to try and protect his little group of family and friends, he was powerless to do anything but watch events unfold.

The other man led a great army and controlled the destinies of thousands of men. In a few hours, this man would make decisions that would send Fountain Branch Carter and his little group into his cellar, hiding in fear, and plunge almost forty thousand men into a firestorm that would, for those who survived, be the raw material of nightmares for the rest of their lives. One Union soldier would later write these words in a letter home:

Franklin Tennessee: These are words that will haunt me the rest of my life.[4]

In this, he would not be alone.

Chapter 1

THE CONFEDERATE ARMY
OF TENNESSEE

September 25, 1864
Palmetto, Georgia

It was a rainy Sunday in this small town, about twenty-five miles southwest of downtown Atlanta, when the stern-looking fifty-six-year-old gentleman stepped off the train and into the red Georgia dirt that had turned to mud. Palmetto was currently the headquarters of what remained of the Confederate Army of Tennessee, and the gentleman was Jefferson Davis, president of the Confederate States of America. After four months of fighting and retreating across northwestern Georgia, the Army of Tennessee had been forced to abandon Atlanta three weeks earlier. There was dissension within the upper command structure of the army, which translated into morale problems in many of the units. Because of the loss of so much war matériel with the fall of the city, the army was short of everything, and finally, there was no agreement on what to do next. The situation with the Army of Tennessee was serious enough that President Davis had come from Richmond, itself now under siege from Ulysses S. Grant's Federal troops, to address these problems in person.

Like Abraham Lincoln, his counterpart in the North, much of President Davis's time was taken up dealing with military issues. Unlike Lincoln, whom many military men in the North considered a meddling amateur, Davis had solid military credentials, both on the administrative side and as a combat soldier.

Other than about eighteen months of formal schooling, Lincoln was mostly self-educated, and his only military experience was a few months as captain of a militia company in the Black Hawk War in 1832. Jefferson Davis's education included studies at two different colleges before entering the U.S. Military Academy and graduating as a second lieutenant in 1828. Davis served on active duty for seven years before resigning his commission to marry the daughter of his commanding officer. During the Mexican-American War, Davis reentered the military, raising a regiment of volunteers from Mississippi and commanding them in combat where he was wounded in action. After the war, he served as the secretary of war for President Franklin Pierce and was serving as a senator from Mississippi when it seceded from the Union in January 1861.

Jefferson Davis came home to Mississippi assuming that he would, for the third time, become a soldier. Unlike some in the South, Davis never believed that separation from the North would be easy. He told everybody who would listen that they should prepare for a long and bitter war. Governor J.J. Pettus commissioned Davis a major general to command the state's militia and then told him to go home and await his orders. When Governor Pettus ask what other preparation he should make, Davis told him to start buying weapons—as many as he could afford.

On February 10, 1861, Davis and his wife Varina were walking in their garden at Brierfield, their plantation south of Vicksburg, when a telegram arrived. It was Davis's marching orders, but not the kind he expected. Mrs. Davis later said that he read the telegram like a man looking at his death sentence. It read:

> *Sir:*
>
> *We are directed to inform you that you are this day unanimously elected President of the Provisional Government of the Confederate States of America, and we request you to come to Montgomery immediately. We also send a special messenger. Do not wait for him.*
> *R. Toombs   R. Barnwell Rhett*

Davis was not to be a soldier after all. He left for Montgomery the next day. As his train stopped along the way, he spoke to the people and told them the same thing he had told Governor Pettus—prepare for a long and bloody war—but in the excitement of the creation of a new nation, they didn't believe him.[5]

The Confederate Army of Tennessee

All that had been three and a half long years earlier, and Davis had seen some of his gloomiest predictions come true, but the problem at hand was the Army of Tennessee. The army had gone through three commanders in the past year. General Braxton Bragg had lost the support of his officers and was replaced by General Joseph E. Johnston on December 27, 1863. Johnston was loved by his men and respected by most of his officers, but he lost the support of the government in Richmond by his constant retreating and was replaced by General John Bell Hood on July 18, 1864. With a mandate to take more aggressive action to defend Atlanta, Hood had launched several attacks and taken over thirteen thousand casualties in the past two months, but in the end he lost the city anyway.

In later years, many would criticize Hood for being too aggressive, and often rightly so, but they sometimes forget that it was his well-earned reputation of aggressiveness that got him the job in the first place. Jefferson Davis and the government in Richmond were looking for someone to go on the offensive after Joe Johnston's months of retreat, and in John Bell Hood they got exactly what they wanted—and more, as it tragically turned out.

President Davis sat down with General Hood to discuss the situation, but he also had meetings with Hood's senior subordinates and asked their opinions. All of them felt that General Hood should be replaced, either by bringing back General Johnston or perhaps with General P.G.T. Beauregard. One of Hood's subordinates went even further. Major General William J. Hardee, the senior corps commander, simply said that he couldn't serve under Hood anymore. Hood had been promoted over Hardee for command of the army—Hardee was already a major general when Hood was still a colonel—and things had gone downhill from there. On Hood's part, the feeling was mutual. He had been carrying on a private correspondence with Davis for some weeks now urging Hardee's replacement. Hardee was unhappy with the way Hood used his troops, and Hood was disappointed with Hardee and his men's performance in the field. By the time of Davis's arrival, it was clear to everybody that one of them must go.

The other problems were just as serious. For an army that suffered from shortages of food, clothing and ammunition in the best of times, the losses the Army of Tennessee suffered with the fall of Atlanta were almost catastrophic. Due to confusion concerning Hood's orders—a problem that would continue to plague the army senior command—a train loaded with the army's entire reserve ammunition supply, twenty-eight boxcars' worth, was trapped inside the city and had to be destroyed. Commissary warehouses containing tons of food and supplies had to be abandoned, their doors thrown open to be looted by civilians. The loss of Atlanta itself also meant the loss of a cannon and railroad foundry, a rolling mill, an ironworks, a machine tool factory and a major Confederate arsenal.

In the past four months, the Army of Tennessee had lost forty-eight artillery pieces and over thirteen thousand small arms to enemy action. As recently as ninety days ago, the Army of Tennessee had reported over sixty-five thousand men "present for duty." Two weeks before President Davis arrived, the army reported an "effective" strength of all arms at just over thirty-nine thousand men.

Accurate figures of strength in Civil War armies are notoriously difficult to agree on, especially for Confederate units. This was not only because accurate counts during a rapidly changing situation were next to impossible, but also because the systems used by many commanders to report their status were far from clear. It was not unusual for a commander to disguise his real situation—fudge his numbers up or down—either to look better to his superiors or to mislead his counterparts across the lines by the creative use of terms like "effective" or "present for duty" or "aggregate present." The results were often confusing to both friend and foe, not to mention later historians trying to get a clear picture of the forces. One author contends that the Army of Tennessee's losses during the four-month campaign that resulted in the loss of Atlanta could have been as high as fifty thousand men from all causes.[6] By any measure, when Davis arrived, the Army of Tennessee was a shadow of its former self.

The supply and manpower problems of the army would have to be worked out over the coming weeks, but for now, the officers needed a plan of action. No matter the condition of the army, they knew that they couldn't sit still and let General Sherman, who outnumbered them almost two to one, dictate the next move. That was a recipe for disaster. Both Hood and Davis were aggressive by nature, and now they formed a plan to force Sherman to come to them and hopefully bring him to battle at a time and place of their own choosing. They would try to keep Sherman off balance and maybe shift the odds a little back in their own favor.

The plan that Hood and Davis agreed on was this: Hood would move back into northern Georgia and operate against Sherman's supply line into Tennessee, the Western and Atlantic Railroad from Atlanta north to Chattanooga. This was country they had just fought over back in May, June and July, and they knew it well. The hope was to bring Sherman out of Atlanta with part of his force and draw him into a battle on ground favorable to the Confederates.

If Hood felt that he still couldn't fight to his advantage in northwestern Georgia, he was to then fall back west to even better ground in the Gadsden, Alabama area, near a supply depot that Hood was expected to establish there. As dangerous as it might be, their other alternatives seemed worse.

Davis and Hood's plan, however, depended on William T. Sherman's cooperation. If Sherman didn't take the bait, they would have to wait for his next move. Among the Confederates, opinion as to what Sherman's next move would be was divided. Hood believed a move to the southwest toward Mobile and the ports on the gulf most likely, but Davis feared a move to the east toward Savannah or Charleston. Davis finally secured a promise that, in either case, Hood would follow and strike at Sherman's rear.

When Davis left Palmetto on September 27, this was the plan had Hood agreed to follow. His grand scheme for an invasion of Tennessee, the capture of Nashville and a march to the Ohio River wasn't on the horizon quite yet, but it wouldn't be long in coming.

The day after Davis left, he sent a message back to army headquarters giving his decision on the personnel matters. Hood would be retained as commander. William Hardee got his wish and was transferred east to command the Department of South Carolina, Georgia and Florida, and command of Hardee's corps would go to Tennessean Frank Cheatham. Once that was settled, Hood got the army on the move. The next day, September 29, they started crossing the Chattahoochee River headed north. At this point, the command structure of the Army of Tennessee assumed the form it would keep throughout the Tennessee Campaign. Getting the issue resolved was good, but the new situation still had problems that would follow the army for the rest of the year.

Even with William Hardee gone, problems remained. Hood was not an easy commander to follow. He was a driven man and not on particularly close personal terms with any of his subordinates. There had already been several instances of orders being confused, either as Hood issued them or as his commanders tried to carry them out. Sometimes it was simply a matter of a plan being overtaken by events as things changed quickly on the battlefield, with the on-scene commanders unable or unwilling to use their own initiative to salvage the situation. Sometimes the orders really were confusing from the outset. In any case, the end result was failure, which ultimately reflected on the commander.

John Bell Hood was not a man to accept failure or blame gracefully, and he expected a lot from the men under him. Unfortunately, his command style didn't create an atmosphere in which subordinates felt they could count on his support if they made too many battlefield decisions without his approval. At critical times in the coming Tennessee Campaign, we'll see field commanders hesitate as they go in person or send back to Hood for new orders to meet a changing or unforeseen situation or simply to clarify orders already received.

Some of the problems with the command situation in the Army of Tennessee at the beginning of October 1864 can be blamed on John Bell Hood, his personality, his command style and even his physical disabilities, but to be fair, some of it also can be explained simply by a lack of experience. It takes time for a military organization to build up the efficiency to run smoothly. In Virginia, Robert E. Lee had been commanding the Army of Northern Virginia for two and a half years, and many of his subordinate commanders and staff had been with him all that time. By contrast, as of September 29, 1864, the Army of Tennessee's commander and his three most senior subordinates' time in their present position was as follows:

> *Lieutenant General John Bell Hood, army commander: seventy-three days*
> *Lieutenant General Alexander P. Stewart, corps commander: fourteen weeks*
> *Lieutenant General Steven D. Lee, corps commander: nine weeks and two days*
> *Major General Benjamin Franklin Cheatham, corps commander: yesterday*

It's not that these men were inexperienced soldiers and commanders in their own right—two of the corps commanders (Stewart and Cheatham) were older and just as experienced as Hood. Both had made brigadier general before Hood, and Cheatham had made major general before him, but now they were serving under his command. Both of these men were excellent soldiers and professional enough not to let that keep them from doing their duty, but it takes time to build the trust and communication that lets an organization run smoothly. The Army of Tennessee and its command structure had taken a beating over the last few months, and adding to all this, they were about to find out that their commander's strategy and objectives could change very quickly and with little warning.[7]

Whatever problems there were, they would have to be worked out along the way because, by October 1, the Army of Tennessee was on the move again. It was going into north Georgia to twist General Sherman's logistical tail. Hood had told President Davis that he intended to "lay his claws" on the railroad supplying the Federal army in Atlanta and hang on until he provoked a response.[8]

Chapter 2

WORKING THE PLAN

"Sherman is weaker now than he will be in the future, and I as strong as I can expect to be."

—*John Bell Hood*[9]

When Hood moved the Army of Tennessee into northern Georgia at the beginning of October, his attention was fixed on Sherman and his troops at Atlanta. Another man, however, was already in motion who would eventually preside over the death of Hood's hopes outside of Nashville. Major General George Henry Thomas, along with two divisions, had already been dispatched to Nashville by Sherman when Hood crossed the Chattahoochee River. Although Hood and his army were on Sherman's mind as well, the immediate cause of Thomas's assignment to secure Nashville and middle Tennessee was another Confederate general who Sherman called "that devil Forrest!" For the last ten days, Nathan Bedford Forrest and 3,500 of his troopers had been traveling through northern Alabama and middle Tennessee doing what they did better than anybody— tearing up railroads, burning blockhouses, bridges and trestles, capturing prisoners, liberating horses and mules and generally raising merry hell among the Yankees wherever they went.

George Thomas's job was to secure Tennessee, and a month or so from now, John Bell Hood would become his chief opponent. Now, however, at the beginning of October, Thomas was sent gunning for Bedford Forrest. As he hurried to Nashville to begin pulling together all the forces he would need to defend it, he wired to Lovell Rousseau, the Federal commander at Pulaski, Tennessee:

> *Press Forrest to death…I do not think that we shall ever have a better chance than this.*[10]

Maybe so, but it was still not good enough.

As far as the Yankees were concerned, Nathan Bedford Forrest may as well have been a ghost. Thomas hadn't been in Nashville a week before Forrest was gone, reaching the north bank of the Tennessee River at Florence, Alabama, on October 5. Getting across, however, would take another two days, and this was only accomplished, as one old veteran said, "with considerable disregard for the third commandment." The river crossing also provided an excellent example of Forrest's "hands-on" command style.

Forrest had to use a small fleet of rickety boats and barges to ferry his men and material across the river. Crossing in the last boat, Forrest himself and all the rest were bearing a hand on the oars—except for one lieutenant. When asked why he wasn't helping, the young man said that, as an officer, he didn't think he should be called on for that kind of work when there were enlisted men available. Forrest promptly knocked the young officer overboard into the Tennessee River. After they fished him out, Forrest said, "Now, damn you, get hold of the oars and go to work! If I knock you out of the boat again, I'll let you drown."[11] Small wonder that Forrest was once confronted and actually shot by one of his own junior officers.[12]

George Henry Thomas was something of a rarity in the Civil War. He was a native Virginian and West Point graduate who remained with the Union. Even though, in the beginning, some wondered if he had divided loyalties, Thomas quickly proved himself to be an utterly fearless, superbly competent and dependable soldier. Called "Old Tom" by his West Point classmates, he acquired another nickname while serving as an instructor there several years later: "Old Slow Trot." This was not because he was slow himself, but rather because when his overeager cadets surged out of line during cavalry maneuvers, Thomas would shout "Slow Trot!" to bring them back.[13] Now, ever since he and his men had stood fast as his commander and most of the rest of the Federal army ran for their lives during a battle in northern Georgia in September 1863, he was called "the Rock of Chickamauga."

Sending George Thomas, his old West Point roommate (class of 1840), to Nashville also served Sherman's own interests. He was, at the time, trying to convince his boss, General Grant, to sign off on a plan for his next move, a campaign east from Atlanta to the Atlantic coast at Savannah, Georgia.[14] Grant had so far resisted, and Sherman knew that the only way he would agree was if he felt that Nashville and middle Tennessee were adequately protected. Sherman hoped to convince Grant that Thomas could deal with whatever mischief Hood or Forrest might cause in Tennessee while he was "Marching through Georgia." For the moment, however, Hood and the Army of Tennessee were causing enough trouble right in Sherman's own backyard.

Davis and Hood's plan to draw Sherman out seemed to be working. On October 4, Hood's army began attacking the railroad north of Atlanta. In the next few days, they captured Federal detachments at Big Shanty and Acworth and threatened Allatoona, tearing up the track as they went. Sherman promptly responded by coming north with over sixty thousand men in pursuit. Not willing to risk a head-on confrontation yet, Hood then moved west toward the Alabama line and had his first meeting with his new commander.

President Davis, as part of his reorganization plan, had created the "Military Division of the West," which would control operations in Alabama and Mississippi, as well as parts of Georgia, Louisiana and Tennessee, and to command this new division, Davis had brought in General P.G.T. Beauregard. Having been briefed by President Davis on the plan agreed upon at Palmetto, Beauregard caught up with Hood at Cave Springs, Georgia, on October 9. Hood assured Beauregard that it was still his intention to attack Sherman's supply lines while looking for a place to bring him to battle. Having that settled, Beauregard left to organize a supply base at Jacksonville, Alabama, which had so far been neglected, and Hood and the army headed back north and east for the Western and Atlantic Railroad. Three days later he struck at Resaca and Dalton.

The Federal army kept pressing northward after Hood, always arriving to find destroyed blockhouses and torn-up rails but the Army of Tennessee gone. Sherman had long since tired of this game of cat and mouse, knowing perfectly well what Hood was trying to do. The red-haired Ohio general had no intention of spending the winter chasing John Bell Hood all over creation or trying to garrison every depot and railroad bridge between Atlanta and the Tennessee line. In trying to do that, he told Grant, "We will lose a thousand men each month and gain no result." While that may have been true, it was also part of Sherman's continuing argument in favor of a move instead from Atlanta east to Savannah that he had still not succeeded in getting approved.

The Federal garrison at Dalton surrendered on October 13, and after destroying more track, the Confederates retired west, halting south of La Fayette, Georgia, on the fifteenth. The part of the original plan that Hood had so far failed to follow was that he was to eventually find a place to his liking and turn and fight the main Federal body. After calling a council of his unit commanders, he decided to pass up the opportunity again. When Sherman reached La Fayette on the seventeenth, Hood had moved southwest toward Gadsden, Alabama. Again, Sherman followed, eventually going into camp about thirty miles east of Gadsden to wait for Hood's next move.

So far, Hood had followed the original plan, after a fashion, but after the council at La Fayette, he decided to abandon it completely. On October 21, Beauregard caught up with the army again at Gadsden and was presented with Hood's grander scheme. Hood still hoped to draw Sherman after him and away from Atlanta, but now he intended to cross to the north bank of the Tennessee River at Gunthersville and attack the Federal detachments on the Memphis & Charleston Railroad at Stevenson and Bridgeport. He then purposed to move on into middle Tennessee, capture Nashville, resupply and recruit from the presumably grateful citizens, move on through Kentucky to the Ohio River and possibly even move east and relieve Lee in Virginia. A breathtaking proposal, to say the least.

As this was presented for Beauregard's opinion and blessing, Hood neglected to mention that he had already, two days earlier, wired Richmond directly, as well as General Richard Taylor, the commander of the department he would be entering, stating his intention to move across the river and into middle Tennessee within a few days, completely bypassing his proper chain of command.

As it turned out, Beauregard actually felt that the plan had merit—at least the part about the move into middle Tennessee. As for the larger, grandiose vision of a march to the Ohio, that had been the dream of many Confederates for the last three years, President Davis and Beauregard himself included, but only time would tell. Nevertheless, Beauregard was intrigued. George Thomas had only been in Nashville for three weeks. While the total number of troops under his command was considerable, most of them were, in fact, spread out over several hundred miles in small detachments. Concentrating them for a defense of the capital would take time.

Time, of course, was the key. As far-fetched as the plan might sound, if Hood could move fast, he might actually have a chance. Gunthersville and the river were only about thirty miles away. Beauregard approved the plan with the understanding that speed was of the essence. Every day Thomas grew stronger and better organized. Just to hedge his bets, however, Beauregard insisted that Hood leave behind most of his cavalry under General Joseph Wheeler to keep up the pressure on Atlanta's supply line. In exchange, Hood was promised the services of Nathan Bedford Forrest, who would be sent to meet him in Tennessee. When word was passed in the camps that they would begin to move north the next day, the troops cheered for the first time in a long time. The loudest rebel yells came from the Tennesseans. They were going home.[15]

Chapter 3

CHANGING THE PLAN

"Damn him! If he will go to the Ohio River, I will give him rations!"
                              —William T. Sherman[16]

On October 22, John Bell Hood and the Army of Tennessee left Gadsden, Alabama, bound—so General Beauregard thought—for Gunthersville, a crossing of the Tennessee River and a move east toward Stevenson and Bridgeport. Before the day was over, however, Hood had changed plans again. Bypassing Gunthersville, he turned west in search of another way across the river. Now the army marched through a mountainous area and down into the muddy bottomland. Having cut loose from the supply base at Gadsden, the march was a dismal one. One Confederate artilleryman remembered it this way:

> *We were cut off from our rations, ragged, shoeless, hatless, and many even without blankets; the pangs of hunger and physical exhaustion were now added to our sufferings.*[17]

When they came out into the valley of the Tennessee River, however, things improved—or at least one soldier thought so. A young officer on the staff of General A.P. Stewart, with an eye for the ladies, later wrote that he was

> *glad to see that we are gradually getting into a country where the women are more patriotic, prettier, & use less snuff than in certain portions of N. Ga.*[18]

Four days after leaving Gadsden, this officer, along with the rest of A.P. Stewart's corps, was outside Decatur, Alabama, over forty miles from Hood's original crossing point.

Whatever Hood's reason for changing his plan and turning west, it was a good decision. Crossing the river at Gunthersville and turning east would have been a move that Sherman would have welcomed. He had substantial forces just across the river from Bridgeport and was himself as close to the river as Hood. Sherman believed that catching Hood north of the river would be a far easier proposition.[19] When the Confederates turned west, however, Sherman would not follow. Sitting eighty miles away in his camp in eastern Alabama, he had finally had enough. On the twenty-fifth, it was confirmed by Federal gunboats on the river that the Southerners were working their way downstream, and the next day, Sherman sent the Federal 4th Corps—three divisions under Major General David Sloane Stanley—to Chattanooga with orders to report to General Thomas. On the twenty-ninth, Thomas ordered them to Athens, Alabama, and then, when it was learned that Hood was sending troops across the river at Florence, on to Pulaski, Tennessee, where they finally arrived on November 4.[20]

General Sherman was tired of trying to guess what Hood would do next. He preferred fighting someone like Joe Johnston, who he said was "a sensible man and only did sensible things."[21] By sending Stanley's corps to Thomas, he was moving to meet the new threat and also strengthening his argument that he be turned loose to march east. Two days later, he sweetened the deal by informing Thomas that Major General John M. Schofield and the 23rd Corps would follow Stanley in a few days. On that same day, October 28, when Sherman received confirmation that Hood was at Decatur, Alabama, he immediately gave orders for his own army to turn and march back to Rome, Georgia. This would put him back on the railroad so he could send Schofield's men into Tennessee, as well as judge Hood's reaction to his eastern movement. There was still some chance that Hood would turn back and follow, but Sherman was convinced that he should move east, regardless of what Hood did. If he followed, Sherman could still turn and deal with him, but if Hood insisted on marching north, then let him become George Thomas's problem. Sherman was headed to the Atlantic.[22]

John Bell Hood's seemingly erratic behavior and constant changing of plans was almost as vexing to his own commander, General P.G.T. Beauregard, as it was to his Federal opponents. While Hood worked his way farther and farther west, searching for a crossing of the Tennessee River to his liking, two things grated on General Beauregard's nerves. First of all, Hood was in the field, at the head of his men, but Beauregard was in the rear, trying to cobble together a supply system to support him.

The supply base near Gadsden was now useless, since the army was over one hundred miles away and planning to move farther north. Supplying a new base at Tuscumbia depended on material brought on the Mobile & Ohio Railroad into Corinth, Mississippi, and shipped east from there on the Memphis & Charleston. Unfortunately, because of battle damage, the Memphis & Charleston railroad now ended fifteen miles short of Tuscumbia, so rickety wagons and carts pulled by decrepit teams had to haul the supplies the rest of the way. With this system, Beauregard had to feed and resupply almost forty thousand men and their animals, as well as build up enough reserves to support a move on Nashville, over one hundred miles away.

The Creole General had come along after the plan had already been made, and he correctly blamed a lack of foresight and experience on the part of the planners as the cause of much of his current logistical grief. He later commented:

> *It was easy to discover in the details of the plan evidences of the fact that General Hood and Mr. Davis were not accustomed to command armies in the field, especially armies like ours...much had to be foreseen and much prepared or created.*[23]

The other thing that weighed on Beauregard's mind, maybe more than anything else, was the delay. By October 30, the first of Hood's troops—from Steven D. Lee's corps—were across the Tennessee River at Florence, Alabama, having chased away the small detachment of Federal cavalry that held the town. It seems that Lee's men were well received by the citizens of the town, especially the ladies. About two weeks later, one soldier wrote to his cousin:

> *The ladies of Florence seem to be very devoted to the Southern cause. When the army first crossed, the advanced guard was almost overwhelmed by kisses from the "fair females." One poor Colonel was kissed by every lady in Florence.*[24]

S.D. Lee's corps was now about one hundred air miles from the Tennessee capital, with nothing between them and Nashville but a few scattered cavalry units and infantry outposts. Under ideal conditions, a week's march could have put them on George Thomas's doorstep, where he held Nashville with only eight thousand garrison troops.[25] As for the Federal army that they would eventually face at Columbia and Spring Hill and Franklin, the lead elements of David Stanley's 4th Corps were still five days away from their point of concentration at Pulaski, Tennessee, and most of John Schofield's 23rd Corps was still camped at Rome, Georgia. It would be two more weeks before Schofield arrived in Pulaski to take command, and even then, all his troops would not be in place.[26] In short, at the end of October, southern middle Tennessee was wide open, if Hood could only have taken it.

One corps, however, was not an army, and ideal conditions only exist in the laboratory. Two-thirds of Hood's men were still on the south side of the river, and Forrest's cavalry, which had been promised, was ninety miles away in west Tennessee. There was still a window of opportunity open for Hood and his army, but it was growing smaller every hour. Federal gunboats were on the river and cavalry patrols regularly came down from Tennessee. The enemy knew where Hood was and almost certainly had guessed his intentions. It was now a race, with Nashville and middle Tennessee as the prize. Unfortunately for Hood, once he reached Tuscumbia, things seemed to grind to a halt.

The energy, drive and aggressiveness John Bell Hood was famous for seem to desert him for a while at Tuscumbia. He had immediately thrown Steven D. Lee's corps across the river and secured Florence on the north bank, but then things seemed to bog down—literally as well as figuratively. Hood, who could push an army as hard as anyone, marching them on empty bellies, now became concerned with resting and refitting his men. To be sure, they were exhausted and dressed in rags and needed almost everything, but this hadn't prevented other movements in the past. It is even possible that the enormity of the gamble he was about to take finally gave him pause. Whatever the reason, when Beauregard finally caught up with Hood at Tuscumbia on November 3, both Stewart's and Cheatham's corps still sat on the south side of the river. The Creole could almost hear the clock ticking and feel the opportunity slipping away. Unknown to both men, the day before, General Grant had finally agreed to turn Sherman loose for what would become known as his "March to the Sea." The issue was now between Hood and Thomas—winner take all.

A general as aggressive as John Bell Hood necessarily depended on a good deal of luck, but at Tuscumbia luck seemed to turn against him for a while, at least where Mother Nature was concerned. The weather, which had been generally good through the last half of October, turned nasty as November opened. Cold wind and rain made life miserable for man and beast, and a rising river washed away camps and plagued the engineers trying to lay a new pontoon bridge. To make matters even worse, just as the bridge was finished, some Union men managed to sneak in and cut loose some of the pontoons, which floated away, causing another three-day delay. All in all, it was two weeks before Cheatham's corps and the supply train was able to cross to the north side of the river. Then another storm blew in and closed everything down for five more days. The one bright spot was that, during this last delay, Forrest and his troopers finally began arriving.[27]

On October 21, when Beauregard had promised Forrest's services to Hood in return for most of Wheeler's cavalry, he thought that Forrest was still in the Corinth, Mississippi area, where he and his men had gone to rest and refit after their raid into middle Tennessee at the end of September. Getting him moving east to link up with Hood should have been a fairly straightforward operation. Unknown to either Beauregard or Hood, however, Forrest was instead in Jackson, Tennessee, five days into a new operation. The order to join Hood arrived several days later, with the instructions to finish his current operation as soon as possible.

After attacking Federal shipping on the Tennessee River near the Kentucky line—and spending a day or so operating his own mini navy with captured river craft—Forrest and his men arrived, undetected, on the west bank of the river opposite the huge Federal river port, supply depot and railhead at Johnsonville, Tennessee. On November 4, Captain John W. Morton, commanding Forrest's artillery, rolled his ten fieldpieces into position, and at precisely 2:00 p.m., all of his guns opened fire. The Yankees were taken completely by surprise, and for the Rebel gunners, it was a turkey shoot. It was so much fun that Forrest and some of his staff tried their hand at loading and firing one of the pieces, to the great amusement of the regular artillerymen. At one point, Forrest was heard to say, as he tried to correct the aim, "Elevate the breech of that gun a little lower." On the Federal side, it was devastation, but for the Confederates, a good time was had by all.

Once all of the gunboats, steamers and barges that jammed the wharf were sunk or disabled, the gunners went for the buildings stocked with supplies and the acres of other material stored on open ground until it could be transferred to rail cars for the run into Nashville. Confederate cavalrymen lined the banks, cheering like it was a ballgame, as the supply dump went up in flames. The cheers were soon mixed with groans, however, when one of the guns set fire to a warehouse on high ground, which turned out to be filled with several hundred barrels of whiskey. A river of flaming liquor ran down the hill, which made a lovely blaze, but everyone agreed that it was a terrible

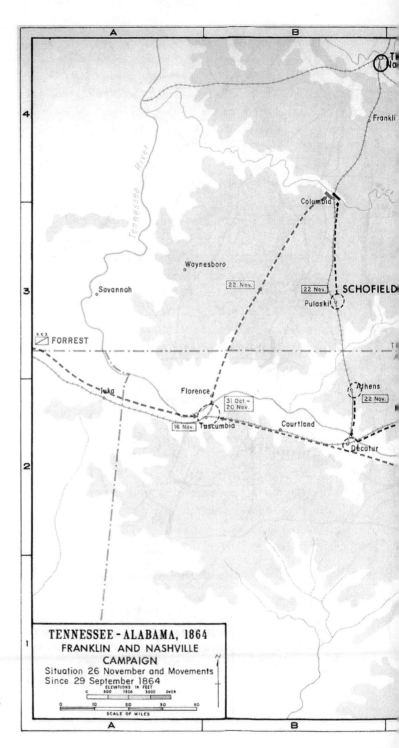

Beginning
the Tennessee
Campaign.
*Department of History,
United States Military
Academy.*

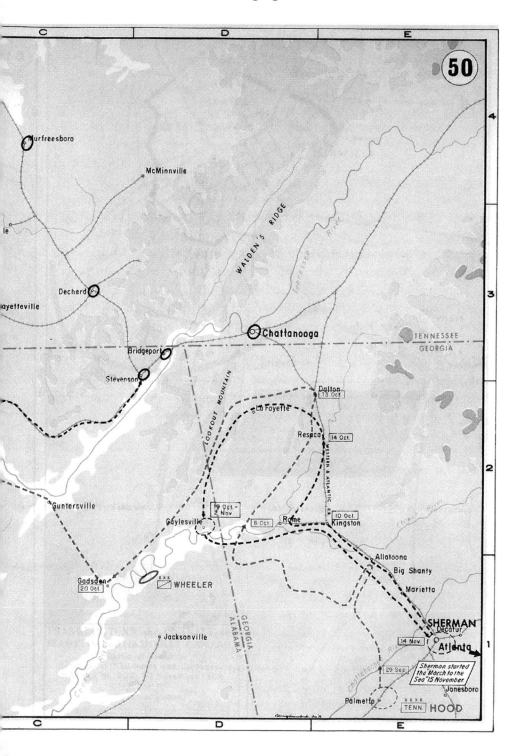

waste of good Kentucky bourbon! When it was all over, Forrest estimated the Federal loss at $6,700,000. His own losses during the entire campaign were two killed and nine wounded.[28]

After burning Johnsonville, Forrest and his men left immediately to join Hood at Florence, Alabama, as ordered, but due to wretched weather, horrendous roads and broken-down horses, it took ten days for them to get there. Meanwhile, Hood and his army struggled to get ready themselves, and General Beauregard fumed. By the time the army was finally ready to move, Beauregard and Hood were barely on speaking terms.

The addition of Forrest and his raiders brought Hood's cavalry strength up to about five thousand riders, which were welcome additions, but it didn't take long for Hood to find out that having Forrest under your command could be a mixed blessing. Soon after Forrest's arrival, Hood issued a general order to the army reducing the numbers of mules per wagon and ordering the extra animals delivered to his quartermaster. Forrest simply ignored the order. The next day, a Major Landis arrived at the general's headquarters, asked why no mules had been sent, and walked into a buzz saw in Forrest.

Nathan Bedford Forrest may not have had the benefit of a classical education like many of the West Point graduates, but when it came to the language the average soldier understood, Forrest's eloquent and extensive vocabulary of profanity was second to none. Captain John Morton, Forrest's chief of artillery, witnessed the encounter between the general and the quartermaster officer and said:

> *The atmosphere was blue for a while. Stripped of General Forrest's bad words, he said to Maj. Landis: "Go back to your quarters and don't you come here again or send anybody here again about mules. The order will not be obeyed; and moreover, if* [the quartermaster] *bothers me further about this matter, I'll come down to his office, tie his long legs into a double bow knot around his neck, and choke him to death with his own shins. It's a fool's order anyway…If he* [Hood] *knew the roads from here to Pulaski, this order would be countermanded. I whipped the enemy and captured ever mule, wagon, and ambulance in my command; have not made a requisition on the government for anything of the kind for two years, and…my teams will go as they are or not at all."*[29]

As far as is known, General Hood wisely let the matter rest.

Finally, after three weeks, all the troops were in place. On November 21, the Army of Tennessee moved out on the Confederacy's last offensive.

Chapter 4

"TENNESSEE'S A GRAVE
OR A FREE HOME"

"The enemy must give me fight, or I will be in Nashville before tomorrow night."
—John Bell Hood to Chaplain Charles T. Quintard, November 29, 1864[30]

All the players were now in place. General John Bell Hood's army was feeling its way north into Tennessee in three columns. To the west, Major General Benjamin Franklin Cheatham's corps marched toward Waynesboro. He commanded three divisions under Major Generals Patrick Cleburne, John C. Brown and William Bate, with Cleburne's division considered one of the Army of Tennessee's best. In the center was Lieutenant General Steven D. Lee's corps of three divisions led by Major Generals Ed "Allegheny" Johnson, Carter L. Stevenson and Henry D. Clayton, headed over backcountry roads to Henryville. On the right, on the road to Lawrenceburg, was the third corps led by Lieutenant General Alexander P. Stewart with divisions commanded by Major Generals Edward Walthall, Samuel French and William M. Loring.

On paper, the three infantry corps reported an "aggregate present" of just over forty thousand men, but the effective total (armed troops actually present for duty) was actually nearer twenty-eight thousand. In addition, Major General Nathan Bedford Forrest commanded three cavalry divisions, led by Brigadier Generals James R. Chalmers, Abraham Buford and William H. "Red" Jackson—about five thousand troopers. Chalmers was to the west while Buford and Jackson were on the Lawrenceburg road, sparring with Federal cavalry and screening the movements of the army. As he moved into

Major General James Harrison Wilson, commander of the Union cavalry during the Tennessee Campaign. *Library of Congress.*

Tennessee, Hood's army's effective strength was about thirty-three thousand men of all arms, plus another four thousand or so unarmed support troops.[31]

The best of the roads were awful, with axle-deep mud in many spots, and the worst, the one assigned to S.D. Lee's center column, abysmal, being a country lane barely able to carry local traffic let alone thousands of men, wagons and animals. The weather didn't let up either. The cold wind, rain, sleet and occasional snow tormented the men, many of whom still lacked blankets, coats and footwear. General Cheatham had actually ordered his men without shoes to make them out of beef hides, turning the hair to the inside and stitching up the leather. They were said to be fine to walk in but didn't smell too good after a few days.[32] Still the men moved steadily on. Some of the Tennessee men were marching through familiar neighborhoods and were just glad to be back home.

The Federal army, whose job it was to watch the Confederates and delay, as best they could, any move they made to the north, had its infantry concentrated at Pulaski, Tennessee, which put them over fifteen miles east of the nearest Confederate column. The Federal 4th Corps, commanded by Major General David Sloane Stanley, had been the first on the scene. With three divisions commanded by Brigadier Generals Nathan Kimball, George D. Wagner and Thomas J. Wood, Stanley had been in place about two weeks. Just over a week ago, Major General John M. Schofield arrived with the 23rd Corps consisting of two divisions under Brigadier Generals Thomas H. Ruger and Jacob D. Cox. In addition, cavalry units under Brigadier Generals John Croxton and Edward Hatch were sparring with Forrest's units east of the Lawrenceburg road and Colonel Horace Capron's brigade was west of Mount Pleasant. Just as the Confederates began to move north, Major General James H. Wilson arrived to take over command of the scattered cavalry units. On November 13, Schofield assumed command of all forces, which his commander, General Thomas, estimated at twenty-five thousand troops of all arms.[33]

For three days, the Confederates marched north and the cavalry skirmished, with the Yankee riders being roughly handled by Forrest's veterans. By the evening of the twenty-third, the Federal infantry had begun to fall back north from Pulaski to Columbia; Hatch and Croxton's men were being pushed east from Lawrenceburg; and Capron's cavalry had been driven north through Mount Pleasant. Early on the morning of the twenty-fourth, Capron was routed again and was soon in full retreat up the pike toward Columbia. Only the timely arrival of Schofield's lead infantry division under Jacob Cox, who blocked the pike and turned back James Chalmers's pursuing Confederate troopers, saved Capron's men and kept Forrest from riding into Columbia, which was garrisoned by a single Federal brigade.[34]

Having lost the sprint up the pike to capture Columbia, Hood spent the next two days bringing up the rest of his force. He sent S.D. Lee with two of his divisions to confront the Yankees directly in Columbia and held the rest of his force out of sight behind a ridge south of town. On the evening of the twenty-seventh, two things happened. General Schofield notified Thomas in Nashville that he was falling back across to the north side of the Duck River, and General Hood held a meeting with his commanders at Beechlawn, the home of Mrs. Amos Warfield.

General Hood explained that he wanted to swing most of his army around the Federal left flank, and to do this, they had to find a suitable crossing on the Duck River and move the Federal cavalry, which was now guarding the fords, out of the way. This first phase of the operation would be General Forrest's job. By daylight, Schofield had crossed the Duck River and taken up positions on a ridgeline on the north bank, while Confederate cavalrymen began to move across the same stream at four different places east of town. All day, Forrest pushed the Yankee riders back from the river and northeast along Lewisburg Pike. General Wilson, the Federal cavalry commander, was convinced that Forrest was headed up the pike to Franklin and ordered a concentration at Hurt's Crossroads. Meanwhile, Confederate engineers had found a crossing point for the infantry at Davis Ford, and with the enemy cavalry gone, they spent most of the day preparing the approaches and getting pontoons in position.

Forrest had done his job well. He had moved most of the Federal cavalry north and east and out of the coming fight. The Duck River was now unguarded east of town, and Schofield's cavalry—his eyes and ears—were out of position to observe the Confederates' next move.[35]

Reports of the fighting east of Columbia and north of the river had been coming in to Schofield's headquarters in the afternoon, and he had sent word to Thomas in Nashville asking for instructions. As the sun went down on that Monday, there was the real sense in the Federal camp that Hood and his Rebels were up to something.

John Schofield finally heard from his cavalry commander in the early hours of November 29, and it wasn't good news. General Wilson confirmed Forrest's movements of the twenty-eighth, gave some reports from prisoners and advised Schofield to withdraw to Spring Hill as soon as possible. Forrest was across the river, and Hood, with the infantry, would be close behind. Still waiting to hear from Thomas in Nashville with instructions, however, Schofield hesitated.[36]

In many ways, Schofield and Hood were opposites. Hood was often impulsive and sloppy in his planning, while Schofield was much more methodical and careful and usually tried to hedge his bets, which is what he did now. He decided to wait a little while with part of his force in front of Columbia until the situation cleared up somewhat—or until he heard from Thomas—but he began pulling in his outposts. He also got his baggage and supply trains—eight hundred wagons long—moving north, just in case. About daylight he sent General David Stanley and two of his three divisions marching north toward Spring Hill, escorting his wagons and reserve artillery. Not having any cavalry available, he then sent an infantry brigade marching east up the north bank of the Duck River to check on the reports of Confederate infantry crossing there.[37] To add to the confusion, just after sunrise, Steven D. Lee's men opened an artillery barrage from the south side of the river, designed to convince the Yankees that the whole Confederate army was still facing them. Before long, however, Schofield knew that this was not true.

Before daylight, John Bell Hood had his battered body in the saddle. His engineers had worked all night laying the pontoon bridge at Davis Ford, and now Hood rode across with General Frank Cheatham at the head of three divisions, beginning his "end run" of Schofield's army. Following immediately would be General A.P. Stewart and his three divisions, and finally, a division borrowed from Lee's corps—at least twenty thousand men in all. In front of them lay over fifteen miles of twisting country lanes before they reached their objective, the little village of Spring Hill on the Nashville Pike. Soon, this long column of gray would be seen by the infantry reconnaissance patrol, and by 11:00 a.m., Schofield knew for certain that he was being outflanked, but where were they going? Were they going to turn and hit him here at his present position or move farther north? He didn't know.

In recent years, there have been questions raised as to Hood's real motive for his flanking move. Some say that he intended from the start to trap the Union army and destroy it at Spring Hill, while others contend that he simply meant to outrun them to Nashville. To do either one, however, he had to gain possession of the pike at Spring Hill, and that was today's objective.[38]

Major General James Wilson, with most of General Schofield's cavalry, had been engaged with Nathan Bedford Forrest's troopers all the previous day and had been pushed north and east up the Lewisburg Pike, going into camp at Hurt's Crossroads after dark. In fact, Wilson had little hope of holding the place, so before sunup, he began withdrawing farther north to Mount Carmel. This was just what Forrest wanted, since he had a surprise in store for the Yankees that morning. Leaving just enough of a force to press the Federal cavalry up the pike, Forrest took another group around behind them, and just as Wilson reached Mount Carmel, he got hit from two sides. The Federal troopers were able to fortify the place and hold off the Confederates, but after a sharp little fight, the gray riders disappeared. Wilson was now convinced more than ever that Forrest was trying to get around him and make a dash up the pike for Franklin and Nashville, so he continued to fall back trying to prevent it. This was, in fact, exactly what Forrest had been working for since yesterday. Wilson had now taken himself and most of Schofield's cavalry out of the real fight, which would begin soon, several miles to the west. Forrest left one brigade to keep encouraging the Bluecoats up the pike and then turned west with the rest of his men on the Mount Carmel Road toward Spring Hill, only five miles away.

Spring Hill, Tennessee, was a small village about halfway between Columbia and Franklin, on the main road and railroad south from Nashville, but it had already seen its share of the war. There had been a battle near there in March 1863, and then it became the headquarters of Confederate cavalry commander General Earl Van Dorn until he was killed in his own office by a jealous husband a few months later.

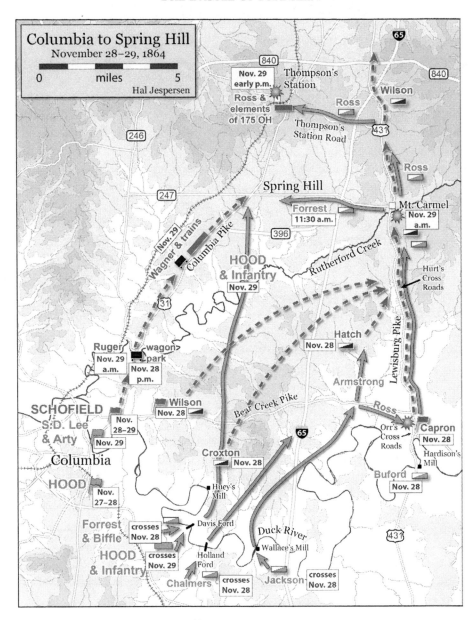

When November 29, 1864, dawned, Spring Hill was just an outpost on the pike manned by the 12th Tennessee Cavalry, a new Federal unit with no combat experience. Their job was to maintain pickets on the local roads and run a dispatch service between Franklin and Columbia, a distance of about twenty-two miles. This morning, however, the town began filling up. Dribs and drabs of different units began to come in from several directions.

By late morning, the head of the long wagon train from Columbia began to arrive, escorted by several companies of Illinois and Ohio infantry. Trotting up the pike alongside the wagon train also came elements of the 3rd Illinois and 11th Indiana cavalry who had been pulled back from picket duty on the Duck River fords west of Columbia. Finally, from the east came a wandering company of the 2nd Michigan Cavalry, who had been separated and cut off during the fighting with Forrest the day before along Lewisburg Pike. Somehow, they had managed to work themselves west during the night and rode into Spring Hill just happy to be alive. It was a grab bag of small detached units, many searching for their larger commands, but Lieutenant Colonel Charles C. Hoefling, in charge of the tiny garrison at Spring Hill, would very soon thank his lucky stars for every one of them.

About 11:00 a.m., just as the last of these units was trying to work its way through the traffic jam of wagons and teams in the town, word came to Lieutenant Colonel Hoefling from his pickets out on the Mount Carmel Road that a large force of Confederate cavalry was approaching. Hoefling frantically gathered up all the bits and pieces of the units in town and sent them east to defend as best they could. Nathan Bedford Forrest had arrived.

About two miles east of town, Forrest's skirmishers began to encounter the Federal pickets but were able to move them back with relative ease, causing Forrest to think that the town might only be held with a small force. Hoping to "keep up the scare," as was his motto, he formed up Frank Armstrong's Mississippi Brigade and parts of two other units and ordered an attack up the road. As they chased the pickets up some high ground, however, they got a nasty surprise. Lieutenant Colonel Hoefling's little ragtag army had moved quickly into a good position on the hill, and many of the Yankees latecomers were combat veterans with breechloaders or Colt revolving rifles. As the pickets ran into their lines, the Federals with their superior weapons opened fire and stung the pursuing Confederates badly, causing them to fall back and regroup.

One little setback, however, didn't slow Forrest down in the least. He immediately sent another unit around to flank the Federal position, only to have them get a bloody nose as well. The wayward Company "M" 2nd Michigan Cavalry, which had escaped capture the day before, now arrived on the scene and pitched into the flanking Confederates with their seven-shot Spencer repeaters. The thrown-together defending force was giving a good account of itself, but it couldn't last. Forrest had over four thousand troops, so the best the Northern soldiers could do was fall back slowly, hoping that the men back in town were using the time wisely. As it happened, they were.

By noontime, Spring Hill was alive with activity. General George Wagner had his division, which had been with the wagon train, double timing the last mile or so into town. Two brigades would be there within a few minutes—Emerson Opdycke's to the north to protect the wagon park and John Q. Lane's stretching the line east of town. These two units arrived just in time to drive off the Confederate skirmishers who were following the Mount Carmel defenders as they fell back into town. It had been a near thing. A few minutes later, and Forrest would have been among them for sure, but in the end, he lost the race to Spring Hill.

For the next few hours, all Forrest and his troopers could do was skirmish and probe the Federal position, which grew stronger with the addition of Wagner's third brigade under Brigadier General Luther Bradley and most of the army's reserve artillery. Bradley covered the southeast sector, which included Rally Hill Pike, the most likely avenue of approach for Hood's infantry.

Forrest had done all he could. His men were exhausted, and since they had to leave their supply wagons back in Columbia, they were almost out of ammunition. After fighting for the last day and a half, most units were down to just three or four rounds per man. All he could do was hold on and wait for the infantry.

Chapter 5

SPRING HILL

"It was the most critical time I have ever seen."
—Brigadier General Luther Bradley, brigade commander,
Wagner's Division, wounded at Spring Hill [39]

After trudging over small country lanes and slogging through muddy fields for eight hours, the head of Hood's column reached Rally Hill Pike, where it crosses Rutherford Creek about 3:00 p.m. The leading division under General Patrick Cleburne waded the creek and hurried on up the pike another mile, where General Hood personally put them in position, with orders to advance and take possession of the pike. He had Cleburne's three brigades aligned facing almost due west, with Mark Lowrey's on the right, Hiram Granbury's on the left and Daniel Govan's in the center, slightly to the rear as reserves. Over three thousand strong, they stepped off from Rally Hill Pike about 3:45 p.m. It was an hour before sundown, and they were just over one mile from the Columbia Pike with nothing in front of them but rolling hills and open fields. Once he had seen Cleburne off, Hood rode back down Rally Hill Pike and established his headquarters at the home of Absalom Thompson.

Less than an hour earlier, twelve miles south at Columbia, Major General John Schofield had finally become convinced that the Confederate flanking move he'd known about for some hours was aimed not at the rear of his position at Columbia, as he first feared, but farther north at Spring Hill, in spite of Steven D. Lee's continuing artillery demonstration from across the river. Knowing now that his army was strung out for over ten miles along the road with at least two-thirds of the enemy force in his rear, Schofield decided that it was time to go. Just as Cleburne's men were stepping off toward the pike just south of Spring Hill, Schofield was leaving Columbia at the head of two brigades commanded by Brigadier General Thomas Ruger. The rest of the troops at Columbia were ordered to withdraw as soon as it was dark, but the real fighting at Spring Hill would be over by the time Schofield got there. It was the Federal 4th Corps commander, General David Stanley, who would actually conduct the battle.

Back at Spring Hill, Patrick Cleburne and his men had been rushed into position so quickly that he had no time for a proper reconnaissance. General Forrest was there as well—one of his brigades would go in on Cleburne's right, even though they had almost no ammunition—but he had little useful information either. As a result, Cleburne and his men didn't really know where the Yankees were, but as they marched across the fields toward the pike, they soon found out. Before they were halfway to the road, the right flank of Cleburne's line—Mark Lowrey's brigade—came to a wooded area, where they were fired upon by Luther Bradley's Federal brigade, which was in position in the trees supported by a section of Pennsylvania artillery. Like the veterans they were, Lowrey's men smoothly changed their front to the right and came straight at Bradley's line. General Cleburne personally brought up Govan's reserve brigade on Lowrey's left, and within a few minutes, Bradley and his men were outflanked and running for their lives back north toward the town. Granbury's brigade on the left continued straight ahead for a while and actually got to within two hundred yards of the pike before turning north themselves, overrunning a Federal regiment and driving them, along with the Pennsylvania artillery, back into Spring Hill.

Patrick Ronayne Cleburne was born in County Cork and served in the British army before coming to America in 1849, and now his Irish blood was up. Abandoning the push to the west for the pike, Cleburne and his men chased Bradley's disorganized crowd through the trees, across a little stream and toward a small hill at the edge of town. It was at this point, winded from the chase and somewhat disorganized, that Cleburne's men saw the cannons. During the afternoon, General David Stanley had used the reserve artillery sent with the supply column to take advantage of a spot of high ground on the southeast edge of town owned by Martin Cheairs. At the rear of Cheairs's fine home (General Earl Van Doren's former headquarters), which still stands and is now called Ferguson Hall, Stanley had established a defensive line on the crest of the hill supported by several batteries of artillery. Bradley's survivors got behind the barricades, and the eighteen guns opened up and stopped the Southerners cold. As they fell back to regroup, one shell even wounded General Cleburne's horse.

It was now about 4:30 p.m., a few minutes before sundown. Almost ten thousand Confederates were on the field, some of them within two hundred yards of the Columbia Pike, which was their primary objective. Within two miles of the field, another ten thousand were waiting to be sent forward. In the little village of Spring Hill, the Federal defenders, one division plus bits and pieces of several other units and some artillery—maybe seven thousand men all told—waited for the axe to fall. General Schofield was on the way with two more divisions, but he wouldn't be there for another two hours. At sundown, the situation, seen from behind the Federal barricades, looked grim. What nobody knew, and what nobody on either side would have believed, was that the significant fighting at Spring Hill was already over. Confusion and indecision at the highest command levels of the Army of Tennessee, along with the coming of darkness, were about to snatch defeat from the jaws of almost certain victory.

Once the Confederate infantry arrived on the field, things began to go wrong, and once it started, it seemed that the Confederate commanders were almost powerless to stop the cascade. It began with Cleburne's pursuit of Bradley and his men. Pressing the enemy when he breaks and runs is a natural reaction in the heat of battle. It's doubtful that Cleburne could have stopped his men, even if he had wanted to, but it changed the orientation of the entire division, from west to north, away from their primary objective, possession of the pike.

It continued with John Bell Hood, who left the conduct of the battle to his subordinates. With Hood off the field, responsibility moved on to Cleburne's corps commander, Frank Cheatham, who at the time of Cleburne's engagement was moving another of his three divisions, under John C. Brown, into position on Cleburne's right. Instead of concentrating on the pike, Cheatham seemed to be planning an assault directly on the town and wanted all three of his divisions to coordinate the attack. Just as Cleburne was ready to hit the Yankees in his front again, he received orders from Cheatham to stand down and wait until Brown's division was ready. Cleburne and all of his men were stunned. They believed that this was a critical error. The time to strike was now. They were certain of it. Daniel Govan later wrote that he firmly believed that, if they had not been halted, Pat Cleburne and his men could have broken the Federal line and had

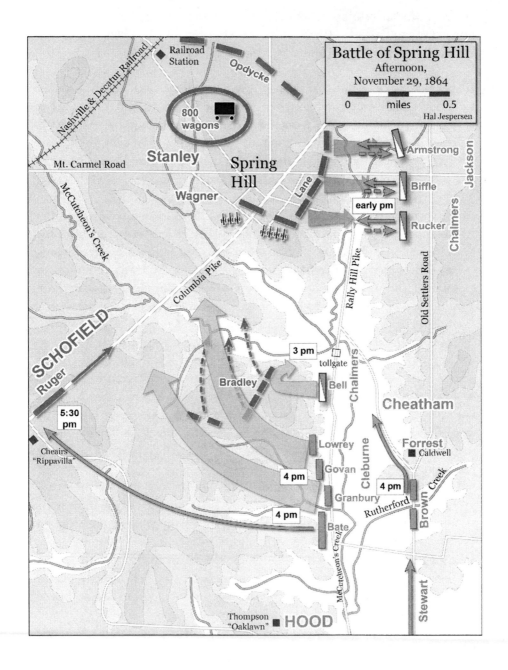

Battle of Spring Hill
Afternoon,
November 29, 1864

0   miles   0.5

Hal Jespersen

possession of the town and the pike in twenty minutes. Optimistic? Maybe, but we'll never know. Cleburne then rode over to find General Cheatham for further orders.

Cheatham's plan was to have John C. Brown's division start the attack on the right, and the sound of his guns would then be the signal for Cleburne to advance. With this ordered, Cheatham rode off in search of his third division under William Bate, only to find that they had been intercepted by General Hood near his headquarters and sent west with the same orders he had given to Cleburne—take the pike. By the time Cheatham found them, Bate and his men had marched through the fields in the twilight and actually struck the pike just north of Rippavilla, the home of Major Nathaniel Cheairs, Martin Cheairs's brother. Just after 5:00 p.m., Bate's sharpshooters were in the process of exchanging fire with the lead elements of General Schofield's column from Columbia when they received orders from Cheatham to move north away from the pike until they made contact with Cleburne's left flank. Given General Hood's orders to him previously, Bate at first refused to comply and asked for confirmation. Cheatham repeated the new orders, not realizing that Bate was actually in position to block the pike. Unknown to both men was the fact that, had Bate been allowed to move across the pike and then been reinforced, fully half the Union army might have been trapped south of Spring Hill. Puzzled as to why they were being told to give up the position they were sent to take, Bate and his men obediently disengaged and stumbled north through the darkness until they linked up with Cleburne's left. All during this time, Frank Cheatham listened for the sound of Brown's guns to tell him that the attack against the town had begun, but it never came.

After meeting with Cleburne and Cheatham, General Brown returned to his division and actually moved his men forward several hundred yards. Before the actual attack started, however, one of his brigade commanders reported enemy troops to the north, and Brown halted his men in place rather than expose his open right flank to attack.[40] This meant that Cleburne never heard the sounds of Brown's guns as a signal to attack, and the coordinated grand assault that Cheatham had planned died in the gathering darkness of confusion and paralysis. Brown sent a staff officer to Cheatham explaining the situation, and Cheatham then took the officer to Hood to repeat his story. By now, it was dark, and Hood reluctantly ordered that the attack should be postponed.

Confusion gave way to frustration as night covered the battlefield. Eventually the Southerners started fires, cooked rations and coffee and bedded down for the night where they were—many of them within a few hundred yards of their main objective, which was left completely open. Some Confederate soldiers said later that they could hear the enemy passing on the pike all night. The two armies were so close together in the darkness that a few Yankee prisoners were actually taken when Federal soldiers coming up from Columbia wandered off the pike and came over to the Confederate campfires looking for a light for their pipes!

Another story illustrates the fact that, if their commander didn't realize that the Federal army was escaping in the darkness, the men on the line certainly did. Two Confederates were eating corn bread around a fire when another soldier walked up and asked their unit. When told that they were with Cleburne's division, the man walked off into the dark. Only then did they realize that he was a Union soldier. "Lets go get him," said one of the rebels, but his buddy replied, "Aw, let him go. If you're looking for Yankees, go down to the pike and get all you want."[41]

Later on, trying to salvage the situation, General Hood sent General A.P. Stewart's entire corps, which never reached the field during daylight, marching over country lanes with orders to block the pike on the north side of town. Unfortunately, Stewart spent several hours wandering in the dark, following one guide only to be overtaken by another officer with what seemed to be conflicting orders and, after riding back to clear all this up with Hood, finally bedded his exhausted men down about midnight without ever reaching his objective. As a last resort, one of Forrest's units, which had captured some ammunition, rode to Thompson Station, a few miles north of Spring Hill, and blocked the pike for a while. They managed to burn a few wagons and scare a railroad engineer half to death when he pulled his train into the station in the middle of the raid, but they didn't stay long. Through all this, John Bell Hood rested at the Thompson home on Rally Hill Pike. Although upset by the confusion, Hood seemed to believe that the Yankees would still be there in the morning and could be dealt with in short order. In this, Hood underestimated his old friend, John Schofield.

While many of the professional soldiers on both sides in the Civil War were acquainted because of prior service together, you don't often see as many close connections as you do at Spring Hill and Franklin.

John Bell Hood and John McAllister Schofield, the field commanders on each side, were no strangers. Eleven years before, they had graduated together in the West Point class of 1853. In fact, they were roommates, with Schofield sometimes serving as Hood's math tutor, which was reflected in their class standing, Schofield being seventh and Hood forty-fourth out of a class of fifty-two. Graduating a year ahead of Schofield and Hood was David Sloane Stanley, currently commanding the defenses of Spring Hill against his old underclassman. Marching up from Columbia with Schofield was one of his division commanders, Thomas Howard Ruger, one year behind both the army commanders in the class of 1854. Ironically, it was one of Ruger's own classmate, Steven Dill Lee, who had just spent part of the afternoon trying to kill him with artillery fire from the south bank of the Duck River at Columbia.

While all these gentlemen were students on the Hudson, their superintendent was Robert E. Lee and their artillery and cavalry instructor was George Henry Thomas, the Federal commander currently waiting in Nashville for the outcome of the battle. John Bell Hood also served with Thomas, Lee and Albert Sidney Johnston in his first active duty assignment with the 2nd Cavalry in Texas. Some of these men's other classmates went on to become Civil War general officers as well, like James B. McPherson, Philip Sheridan, George Washington Custis Lee and J.E.B. Stuart. As with other Civil War battles, Spring Hill and Franklin would be all the more tragic because many of the men there, fighting and dying, were old friends.

After his brush with Bate's sharpshooters on the pike near the Cheairs home, John Schofield rode into Spring Hill about 7:00 p.m. knowing that he was facing the bulk of the Southern army. When the frightened engineer pulled his engine into the Spring Hill depot and told of the Rebels at Thompson Station, Schofield personally marched there with Ruger's division. Forrest's men had gone, so he left Ruger there to keep the road open and rode back to Spring Hill, where he met General Jacob Cox, who had just arrived with the last division from Columbia. Schofield told Cox to lead the way with his troops, and the retreat north to Franklin began, just after midnight. For the next few hours, wagons, cannons, horses and marching men filled the pike headed north. Wagner's division acted as the rear guard, with the last unit to leave, about 6:00 a.m., being Emerson Opdycke's brigade, the first troops to arrive eighteen hours earlier. For a while, no one followed.

At Spring Hill, all of the weaknesses of the command structure of the Army of Tennessee under John Bell Hood became painfully evident. Marching all day and then going straight into battle with only one hour or less of daylight remaining, as happened at both Spring Hill and Franklin, placed great burdens on corps and division commanders and their troops and left almost no room for error.

On a Civil War battlefield, which could cover miles, the situation on the ground can change from minute to minute, but new orders and new intelligence can only travel at the speed of a horse and rider. Confusion was inevitable, and flexibility and improvisation were vital. Sometimes even personal initiative on the part of commanders and extraordinary physical sacrifice on the part of the common soldiers were not enough to overcome a bad situation. Under the best of conditions, it took a tight organization, with mutual respect and trust from the senior commanders down to the men in the ranks, plus a healthy dose of luck, to work through the "fog of war" and win. At Spring Hill, John Bell Hood and the Army of Tennessee seemed to lack both.[42]

Chapter 6

BREAKFAST AT RIPPAVILLA

"He was wrathy as a rattlesnake this morning, striking at everything."
—General John C. Brown on John Bell Hood's temperament at breakfast,
November 30, 1864[43]

T hey were all gone.
        Even with all the problems and missed opportunities the day before, John Bell Hood still seemed convinced that the army under his old West Point roommate would still be there when the sun came up, but it wasn't.[44] Even though he spent the evening at the Thompson home, two miles from the battlefield, Hood received frequent, if sometimes confused, reports from the front. While he was disappointed with what he heard, he still seemed to believe that everything could be resolved the next morning. When he woke up on November 30 and found that the entire Federal army had escaped, he was shocked, and then he was furious.

As Hood and some of his staff rode west across the same fields that General Bate and his men had covered twelve hours before, he sent aides to locate some of his subordinate commanders and order them to a breakfast meeting at Rippavilla, the Cheairs home on the Columbia Pike. Few details of the meeting are known except that the atmosphere was heated and the language was colorful, to say the least.[45] Hood was raging at everybody, with his anger falling first and foremost on Frank Cheatham and his two division commanders, John C. Brown and Patrick Cleburne. That morning, though, whether you felt any personal responsibility for the failure or not, everyone in Hood's army, from the commander to the lowest man in the ranks, knew that a great opportunity had been lost. The only thing to do now was to follow the Federals and hope for another chance.

The missed opportunity at Spring Hill could not help but color the relationship between John Bell Hood and his senior commanders as they marched north after the Northern army, and they shortly faced some critical decisions. In later years, tempers would cool and apologies would be made, but not today. Harsh words had been spoken, and charges were made that proud nineteenth-century Southern men could scarcely abide. Particularly stung by Hood's accusations was Patrick Cleburne. The Irish general was proud of his record, and with good reason. To have it suggested that he might have been derelict in his duty, or even worse, that he and his men might have been too timid in their assault, was almost a mortal insult. Hood would come to Franklin disgusted with his army's performance, even though some of the blame rightly fell on his own head. His corps and divisions commanders, Cleburne chief among them, would come determined to defend their honor and reputation.

The fact that one or another of the Southern commanders may have felt disappointment or betrayed or even insulted did not, however, mean that they could not and would not do their jobs. These were all professional soldiers. As for the men they commanded, any doubts about the Army of Tennessee's courage or willingness to fight—from behind entrenchments or any other way—would soon be washed away in blood.

General Forrest, having scrounged fresh ammunition for his troopers from one of the infantry units, was on the road early. He divided his units into three sections, one going west to the Carter's Creek Pike and another east to the Lewisburg Pike, both then heading north for Franklin, while he took his escort and Tyree Bell's brigade north on the pike to harass the Federal rear guard.[46] By 8:00 a.m., A.P. Stewart's corps, being the farthest north, was on the road, followed by Frank Cheatham's men. S.D. Lee, having just arrived after an overnight march from Columbia, was told to follow with his corps and most of the army's artillery as soon as he was able.

All morning, John Schofield's army marched north toward Franklin, with the rear guard prodding along the stragglers and abandoning wagons whose teams had given out, while Forrest's men nipped at their heels. Two miles south of Franklin, the road climbs a few hundred feet and passes between two hills before dropping down into the Harpeth River Valley.

Breakfast at Rippavilla

It was here, between Winstead and Breezy Hills, that George Wagner's three brigades set up a delaying action, having the high ground and a few artillery pieces. Instead of confronting the Yankees, however, A.P. Stewart led his men east on a country road called Henpeck Lane where, within two miles, they came to Lewisburg Pike. With Stewart on their flank and Cheatham's men coming on, Wagner was forced to pull his men off the ridge, leapfrogging his brigades back north up the pike until he began putting them in position as skirmishers, half a mile in front of the main Union line.

As Wagner and his men fell back, Cheatham and his three divisions filed through the gap and began to spread out on the northern slopes facing the town. On Cheatham's right, A.P. Stewart's men were coming down Lewisburg Pike and doing the same in the fields near the Harpeth River and around a fine old house and plantation named Carnton, owned by John McGavock. As the commanders arrived, they each looked for a vantage point to see what they might be facing. General Hood was one of the first on the north slope of Winstead Hill, intently studying the Federal position on the southern edge of Franklin through field glasses. Frank Cheatham and Pat Cleburne also did their own surveys, as had Forrest some time earlier. After a few minutes, Hood rode back over the hill and down to the home of a family named Harrison on the south slope of the hill, sending aides off to call his other commanders to a meeting.

It didn't take long for Hood's generals to voice their opinion of the situation. It was obvious that since arriving in Franklin the Federals had not been idle. They had all seen the enemy position and didn't like it. Nathan Bedford Forrest was Hood's most successful commander. Forrest and his men had dominated the Federal cavalry in every encounter since they crossed the Tennessee River. He had been the first on the scene at Franklin and had done a thorough reconnaissance. He was also the only one at the meeting who had ever fought over this ground. Eighteen months before, Forrest had ridden and raided over all the area from Columbia, Tennessee, north to Brentwood. If anyone knew the ground, it was Forrest. If anybody's opinion should have carried weight with Hood, it was Forrest. Even before Hood had gotten a chance to see it for himself, Forrest had come back to meet him and said that the Federal line at Franklin was so strong that taking it by assault would be far too costly. Forrest saw a flanking attack as the only reasonable move and had pledged to his commander:

General Hood, if you will give me one strong division of infantry with my cavalry, I will…flank the Federals from their works within two hours time.

Hood, however, didn't see it that way:

I don't think the Federals will stand strong pressure from the front. The show of force they are making is a feint…to hold me back from a more vigorous pursuit.

That was that. Forrest had presented his case and Hood had declined his offer. Instead, Forrest was told to go back to the cavalry and prepare to support the infantry attack by covering the flanks and being ready to press the Federals when they broke and ran for Nashville.[47]

Next to speak up was Frank Cheatham. Knowing that he was under a cloud for yesterday's fiasco at Spring Hill, Frank could have simply deferred to his commander, but he was too much of a professional not to give an honest opinion:

I don't like the looks of this fight. The Federals have an excellent position, and are well fortified.[48]

Hood didn't dispute Cheatham's assessment or claim that it would be easy but said that he would rather fight them here, where they had only had a short time to prepare, than to fight them at Nashville, where they had been fortifying for three years.[49] Left unsaid was the fact that, if the Federals were allowed to escape to the capital, nobody knew how many more troops would be there to join them.

Pat Cleburne was there as well and echoed his corps commander's opinion, adding that he thought a frontal attack would only result in "a terrible and useless waste of life." Forrest again repeated his plea for infantry to support his cavalry in a flanking movement but was turned down a second time. All opinions heard, Hood's decision remained the same. They would attack the main Federal line immediately and drive them "into the river at all hazards."[50]

Chapter 7

NO TURNING BACK

"We will make the fight."[51]
–John Bell Hood about 2:00 p.m., November 30, 1864

In contrast to his plan for a sweeping, complicated maneuver at Spring
Hill, Hood's plan at Franklin was elegant in its brutal simplicity. He would
simply hit them head-on with everything he had. At the beginning of the
attack, he had available on the field two full infantry corps, each composed
of three divisions—eighteen brigades made up of over 120 regiments: nearly
18,000 men. In addition, he had Forrest's cavalry on each flank, something
above 4,000 troopers. Finally, General Ed Johnson's 2,700-man division of
S.D. Lee's corps would arrive after the attack was underway and be sent in
after dark. During the next five hours, John Bell Hood would commit to
battle, somewhere on the field, almost 25,000 men.

After the war, many would criticize Hood for his decision to send his
army to attack the Yankees head-on at Franklin. As the commander on the
field, the blame was rightly his, as would have been the glory if he had
succeeded, and in retrospect his decision can be seen as tragically flawed,
but not for some of the reasons others have given. It's highly unlikely, for
instance, that Hood was unbalanced enough to send his men forward just to
"teach them a lesson," and there is no evidence that he was acting under the
influence of such painkillers as were available. By far the most reasonable
explanation seems to be that Hood simply deceived himself as to what could
be accomplished. His reasoning that he must strike at the Federal army before
they reached the safety of the fortifications at Nashville was quite correct.

To some extent, Hood's attack was an act of desperation. Something had to be done at Franklin before sundown or he would lose his last chance at this Federal army. In fact, General Schofield had already issued orders to begin withdrawing the Federal infantry from the entrenchments and passing them over the river as soon as it was dark if no attack came.

What probably sent Hood's men forward was the same sort of self-delusion that caused Robert E. Lee to send almost twelve thousand men across the field on the third day at Gettysburg, against the pleas of their corps commander, General James Longstreet, who, like Forrest, begged for the chance to try a flanking movement instead. Hood was now about to send over twenty thousand men on a similar mission. Like Lee, Hood had convinced himself, against all advice, that the Federal line would break if hit hard enough in the center. Both Hood and Lee committed cardinal sins of command: they made unreasonable demands on their own men, and they underestimated the strength and courage of their opponent. The price for their clouded vision was, of course, borne by the men on the field. For Lee's part, he immediately realized his mistake and rode among the survivors of Pickett's Charge telling them that it was all his fault. Both circumstances and Hood's personality prevented him from being able to do the same.[52]

Hood's plan would send A.P. Stewart's three divisions forward on the eastern half of the field following the Lewisburg Pike and the Nashville & Decatur Railroad tracks. Covering the right flank next to the Harpeth River would be dismounted elements of Forrest's cavalry. Next would come the division under Major General William Wing Loring. On Loring's left was the division of Major General Edward Cary Walthall, and on Stewart's left flank was the division of Major General Samuel Gibbs French.

Frank Cheatham's corps would cover the western half, with Major General William Bate's division's left flank on the Carter's Creek Pike and dismounted cavalry covering his left. Straight up the middle would come the divisions of Major General Patrick Ronayne Cleburne and Major General John Calvin Brown, with Cleburne on the right of the Columbia Pike, connecting with French's division, and Brown on the left, connecting with Bate.

Some have suggested that Hood put Cleburne and Brown in the center to punish these two divisions for their part in the failed attacks at Spring Hill, but there is no evidence of that. The real reason is probably the most obvious—in spite of what may or may not have happened the day before, these two units were still Hood's best. Between them, Cleburne and Brown could field

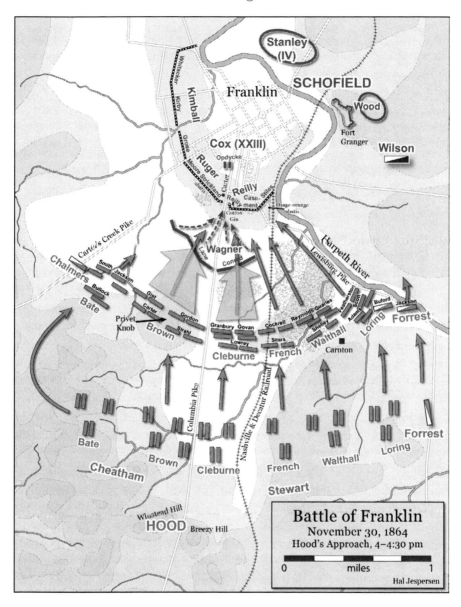

Battle of Franklin
November 30, 1864
Hood's Approach, 4–4:30 pm

0   miles   1

Hal Jespersen

almost seven thousand men. The point where the pike passed through the Federal works would be the critical spot, and if Hood was to have any hope of breaking the enemy line, his heaviest blow would need to fall there. The other obvious reason they drew the assignment was simply because they were there. Cleburne and Brown's men were already on both sides of the pike. To move them anywhere else would have taken time that Hood didn't have.

By 3:30 p.m., Confederate units could be seen from Franklin, falling into line in the open fields to the south. Regimental and division flags were flying and bands were playing. From almost two miles away, it looked like a grand military review to the Federal troops manning the entrenchments on the south edge of town. Even so, everybody realized that this was no parade, so they watched with keen professional interest.

Federal 23rd and 4th Corps Defensive Positions
Franklin, Tennessee, November 30, 1864

Major General John Schofield and Brigadier General Jacob Cox rode into the outskirts of Franklin, Tennessee, about 4:30 a.m. at the head of Cox's division, the vanguard of the Federal army—almost two hours before sunrise. Cox and his men had covered twenty-two miles in ten hours. Cox stopped at the first house he came to, woke up Fountain Branch Carter and his family and established his division headquarters in their front parlor. General Schofield rode on into town in search of his engineering officer, Captain Twinning, whom he had sent on ahead. Above all, Schofield hoped to find railroad cars with pontoons on them. The county bridge over the Harpeth River was known to be out, so Schofield had twice wired General Thomas requesting that he send pontoons down to Franklin to be available for the engineers. Schofield had almost eight hundred wagons to move across the river, the last natural barrier before Nashville, and without pontoons he could well be stuck south of the river all day while Hood and his army caught up. The last thing he wanted was to have to fight with the river at his back.

The soldiers were falling out on either side of the road, filling up Mr. Carter's yard, starting fires and cooking coffee. Jacob Cox and his staff were sprawled all over Mr. Carter's rug in the parlor, trying to catch a few winks of sleep, when General Schofield reappeared and woke him. He had just returned from the river. Over thirty years later, Cox wrote of their conversation:

> *In all my intimate acquaintance with him, I never saw him so manifestly disturbed by the situation he was in…that morning. He spoke with a deep earnestness of feeling he rarely showed. "General," he said, "the pontoons are not here, the county bridge is gone, and the ford is hardly passable. You must take command of the 23rd Corps and put it in position here to hold Hood back at all hazards till we can get our trains over and fight with the*

river in front of us. With Twinning's help I shall see what can be done to improve the means of crossing, for everything depends on it.[53]

So began what was probably Jacob Cox's finest day in a Federal army uniform. General Schofield's engineers would rebuild the washed-out wagon bridge, plank over the railroad bridge and finally begin crossing the wagons over the river that afternoon, but by then, all Jacob Cox's attention would be focused in the opposite direction.

When the war began, Jacob Dolson Cox was thirty-three years old, married, the father of six children and in poor health. Because of political connections, however, he was able to obtain a commission as a brigadier general in the Ohio militia, but unlike some political appointees, Cox turned out to be a solid, dependable soldier. After the war, he would go on to several careers as a public servant, educator, lawyer and writer, but that was all in the future. Today, his job was to defend John Schofield's bridgehead over the Harpeth River.

Around the south edge of Franklin, there were some old entrenchments, dug by the Federal forces a year or so ago, and Cox decided to use them as the basis for his defense. As the troops arrived from Spring Hill, Cox turned them out into this old line and ordered them to improve it as best they could. Cox began with his own division. They were already on hand, having marched in with him, and they were the troops he knew best.

Starting on the east, with their left flank on the Harpeth River, was Cox's third brigade, Indiana men commanded today by Colonel Israel N. Stiles.[54] They stretched from the riverbank and railroad bed on their left to the Lewisburg Pike, covering a front of about 250 yards. Next came the second brigade under Colonel Joseph S. Casement, running from the Lewisburg Pike to a point just in front of Mr. Carter's cotton gin, about 400 yards. Finally, Brigadier General James W. Reilly's first brigade covered the critical area from the cotton gin to the Columbia Pike with two regiments on the line and three more in reserve—a front of about 160 yards. Because of Cox's temporary promotion to corps command, Reilly, as senior brigade commander, took over command of the division as well. Incorporated in this line were eight artillery pieces with twelve more a few hundred yards in the rear.

As Thomas Ruger's division arrived, short one brigade, they were set to work on the fortifications west of the Columbia Pike. Colonel Silas A. Strickland's brigade went in with the 50th Ohio Regiment on the pike linking up with the 72nd Illinois to the west. Sixty-five yards in their rear, running from the pike, behind Mr. Carter's farm office and smokehouse, and down the western slope of Carter Hill, two new regiments began digging a second fallback line. In the two days that the 44th Missouri and the 183rd Ohio had been with Schofield's army, all they had done was march, and they dragged into Franklin having covered twenty-two miles since sundown the day before. Because they were untested and late in arriving, they were put along this second line, the 44th beginning just east of the pike and the 183rd extending the line to the west. Completing the front line from Strickland's brigade to the Carter's Creek Pike was Colonel Orlando H. Moore's brigade, the line west of Columbia Pike being about the same length as the eastern part. This section of the line was supported by ten artillery pieces firing from Carter Hill and four more near the Carter's Creek Pike.

The balance of the Union infantry—the 4th Corps under Major General David S. Stanley—was divided into three sections. One division under Brigadier General Thomas J. Wood was sent across the river via the ford and the railroad bridge to act as a covering force, able to protect the bridges and guard the wagons after they had crossed. Brigadier General Nathan

The Carter cotton gin and press house as seen from Columbia Pike, circa 1880. Cleburne's division attacked up the road in the foreground. Major General Patrick Cleburne was killed between the fence and the gin house. *U.S. Army Military History Institute.*

Kimball's division was sent to extend the front line west of Carter's Creek Pike on to the Harpeth River northwest of town, throwing up barricades using whatever material was at hand, while Brigadier General George Wagner's division acted as the army's rear guard. Finally, General Wilson and the cavalry had reestablished contact and were on both sides of the river east of town, ready to counter any flanking move by Forrest. Of these troops, almost all of the heavy fighting would be done by the two divisions of the 23rd Corps in the mainline and George Wagner's division from the 4th Corps, almost fifteen thousand men in all.[55]

Few Civil War battlefields offered such an unrestricted view of the ground in front of the defenders as Franklin. Open fields with only a few groves of trees stretched out in the Union army's front for two miles, and it was over this ground that any attacker must pass. Having troops in the open for so long was an artilleryman's dream and would shortly become the Confederates' nightmare. To make matters worse, while the field started out almost two miles wide, as an attacker got closer to the Federal lines, the Harpeth River began to pinch in on the east so that units on that flank were obliged to shift to their left, crowding others off their original line of advance and mixing regiments and brigades together. It was like marching down into a funnel. When they finally reached the Federal entrenchments, Hood's entire attacking force would be compressed onto a front barely 1,600 yards wide. So many men packed into such a small space, and all fighting for their lives, would shortly produce a level of horror, bloodshed, violence, brutality and hand-to-hand combat beyond the experience of even the most hardened veterans on either side. One Federal officer, defending the line about two hundred yards west of the Columbia Pike, would later simply say, "I thought I knew what fighting was."[56]

Many modern innovations made their appearance in the Civil War, but some things about military engineering hadn't changed in centuries. The Federal entrenchments were classic in design—the best protection for the defender and the most obstruction for the attacker. Julius Caesar had built very similar defensive works two thousand years before in Gaul. For the most part, they consisted of two ditches dug parallel and several feet apart. The dirt from the ditches was thrown to the center. When finished, you had a dirt berm maybe five feet high with a ditch three feet deep or so on the outside and a slightly more shallow one on the inside. This made an eight-foot obstacle for an attacker and a secure shelter for the defender. Trees were cut down to provide timber to put along the top, and underneath these head

Carter cotton gin circa, 1880. Some of the fiercest fighting of the battle took place around this building. It was torn down a few years after this picture was taken. *Carter House Archives.*

logs firing slits were dug out. In front of the works, more obstructions were built out of whatever was available. On the eastern end of the line, a long hedge of Osage orange trees (also called Bois D'Arc) ran less than fifty yards in front of Stiles's brigade. These trees, which contained long thorns on their branches, were cut off about four feet above the ground and the tops used to extend the line of thorn bushes to the right, in front of Casement's men. Any attacker would have to stop within easy rifle shot and, in full view of the men in the trenches, work their way through a thorny thicket before being able to storm the works.[57]

On the west side of Columbia Pike, a grove of locust trees served much the same purpose—anything to break up the momentum of an attacking force and make them an easier target. Only in the center, from in front of Mr. Carter's cotton gin west to the locust grove, was the ground relatively unobstructed all the way to the mainline of entrenchments.[58]

Shortly after noon, the work on the Federal lines was largely finished, and the men began to relax, cook rations, smoke or sleep. At Fountain Branch Carter's house, two families of neighbors had come with their children, knowing that Carter had a basement for shelter in case of trouble. One of the families lived on the other side of Columbia Pike just north toward town. German immigrants Johann Albert Lotz and his wife Margaretha had bought the house lot from Mr. Carter, and Johann, a master carpenter who did intricate woodwork and built fine pianos, had done most of the work on their house himself. Feeling that Mr. Carter's brick house would be a better shelter than their frame one, however, Johann and Margaretha had brought their three children, Paul, Matilda and Augustus, across the street to weather the storm, if it came. This proved to be a good decision because before long their house would suffer substantial damage from small arms and artillery fire, some of which can still be seen. The Lotz House would also serve, along with the Carter House, as a hospital after the battle. Both houses still stand on Columbia Pike today.

The Lotz House. Home of Johann Albert Lotz, a German immigrant and master carpenter. Lotz and his family lived across the street from Fountain Branch Carter and took refuge, along with other civilians, in Carter's basement during the battle. *Lotz House.*

At least three members of the black families who lived there and worked for Mr. Carter were in the house too. Carter owned twenty-eight slaves at the beginning of the war. When the Federal forces came into the area in early 1862, some of the slaves may have run away, but several were still living in cabins on Carter's property, working on his farm and at the cotton gin. They would not have been automatically freed in 1863 since the Emancipation Proclamation did not apply to Tennessee. By 4:00 p.m., at least twenty-five civilians were inside the Carter house, half of them children.[59]

Chapter 8

IT IS A MISTAKE

"It is a mistake, and it is no comfort to me to say that we are not responsible."
−Major General Benjamin Franklin Cheatham

By 3:30 p.m., John Bell Hood had two of his three infantry corps on the field, with the third under S.D. Lee coming up fast with most of the army's artillery. As much as he would have liked to have had the extra men and especially the cannons, Hood could not wait for them. By the time the men already at hand could get organized and go forward, he would be lucky to have an hour of daylight left, so the order had already been given.

All across the open fields in front of Winstead and Breezy Hills, and east almost to the Harpeth River, six Confederate divisions were on the move. They might be ragged and tired and worn, but they were still professionals and they would act like it. Lines were formed with precision, flags were unfurled and several regimental bands struck up "Dixie" and "Bonnie Blue Flag" as the formations took shape. Mounted officers rode up and down the lines to the cheers of the ranks, and the troops went forward. As they advanced, most divisions would deploy into a formation with two brigades in front and one behind as support.[60]

A mile and a half away, the grand spectacle was watched by the men in the Federal lines, and before long their own bands were replying with their own tunes. General Jacob Cox, riding along behind the eastern flank of his line near the Lewisburg Pike, took a moment to stop and watch the grand spectacle unfolding in the fields in front of him:

...the long lines of Hood's army surged up out of the hollow in which they had formed, and were seen coming forward in splendid array. The sight was one to send a thrill through the heart, and those who saw it have never forgotten its martial splendor...it was a rare thing to have a battlefield on which the contending armies could be seen. [61]

At this distance, the ragged uniforms and the bare feet of many of the Southern men couldn't be seen, but even if they had been, the men in the Federal line would not have been fooled by their looks. They had fought this Confederate army often enough to know that beneath the torn gray coats and the ragged slouch hats were some of the toughest and most dangerous soldiers in the world. In spite of the strong Federal position, the Confederates were coming to attack head-on, and everyone knew that there would be hell to pay. At least the Federal soldiers could take some comfort in the fact that today, unlike most of their battles in the past, they were the ones behind the fortifications.

As the Confederate army moved forward, the gravity and danger of what they were about to do was plain to every man. Earlier, when it had been announced that they would attack, crowds of men in many regiments gathered around their chaplains with requests that they hold something of value for them—a watch or a Bible or a picture or a letter to their family. Like many of the chaplains, James McNeilly of Quarles brigade had to refuse his men since he had decided to go forward with them and share their fate. [62]

Even as they advanced, many of the commanders still had serious misgivings about the attack. Pat Cleburne had ridden forward and inspected the Federal works through a sharpshooter's telescope while his division was forming, and one of his brigade commanders said that he was "greatly depressed." Even so, Cleburne had personally promised General Hood that he would "take the works or fall in the attempt." [63] Frank Cheatham was reported to have indicated that he was sending his men forward almost under protest, saying, "It is a mistake, and it is no comfort to me to say that we [Hood's subordinate commanders] are not responsible." [64]

At the distance of over one mile, it was hard for the men in the mainline to make out much detail in the Southern army, but a few Federal troops had a much better view, and they were getting very nervous. The center of the Confederate line was about to encounter the only real tactical blunder the Federal forces made that day.

It Is a Mistake

Federal Advanced Line
Eight Hundred Yards in Front of the Mainline
3:50 p.m.

Shortly after 2:00 p.m., Colonel Emerson Opdycke and his bedraggled brigade came down Columbia Pike. They were part of General George Wagner's division of the 4th Union Corps and had been the rear guard during the march from Spring Hill. Now that the Confederates held the hills south of town, Opdycke was falling back to the mainline when he met his commander about eight hundred yards in front of the fortifications. Wagner was putting one of his other brigades under Colonel Joseph Conrad[65] in position on the east side of the pike and told Opdycke to take his men and do likewise on the west side. Incredibly, Opdycke refused. In colorful terms, he told Wagner how stupid he thought it was to leave his exhausted men out in such an exposed position and continued riding toward the mainline, his men following along behind. Wagner rode up beside the disobedient colonel, and they argued the entire half-mile to the entrenchments, shouting at each other while the troops along the line enjoyed the show. Wagner finally gave up and said, "Well, Opdycke, fight when and where you damn please! We all know you'll fight." About two hundred yards north of the Carter House, Colonel Opdycke put his men in a field and told them to stack arms and rest.[66]

By 3:00 p.m., Wagner had ridden back and placed his last brigade under Colonel John Q. Lane west of the pike, where Opdycke would have gone. It's fairly certain that both Conrad and Lane had the same opinion of the position as Opdycke. They just didn't seem to have the nerve to defy Wagner to his face. General Wagner's two brigades now formed a three-thousand-man skirmish line across the pike to watch the Confederate advance. It was scary out there, a half a mile in front, but surely they would be withdrawn as soon as any serious attack was imminent. Those, after all, were Wagner's orders.[67]

When Wagner rode back to the mainline for the second time, about 3:30 p.m., the Rebels were almost one mile away from his advanced line and forming up. Now, about twenty minutes later, they were less than half a mile and coming on. A staff officer rode in from the advanced line and asked for orders to retire. Captain Levi T. Scofield, Jacob Cox's engineering officer, was with Wagner and recorded the exchange: "Stand there and fight them!" Wagner said. Then, remembering his disobedient colonel, he added "And that stubbed, curly-headed Dutchman will fight them too!" When reminded that the order was to retire if threatened, Wagner said nothing.

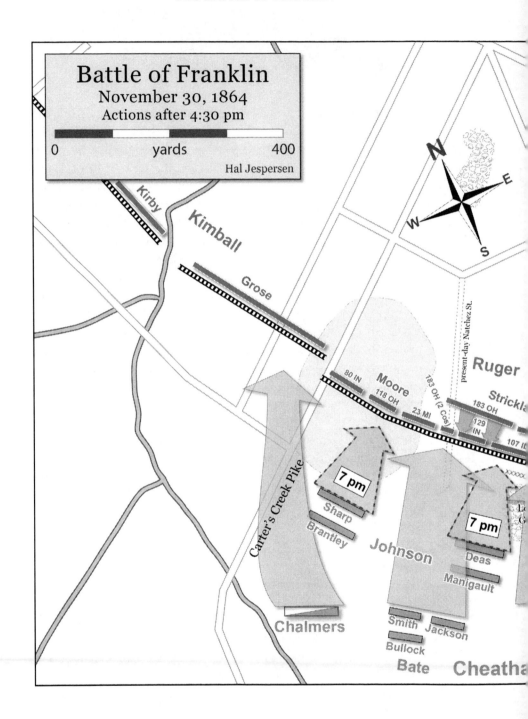

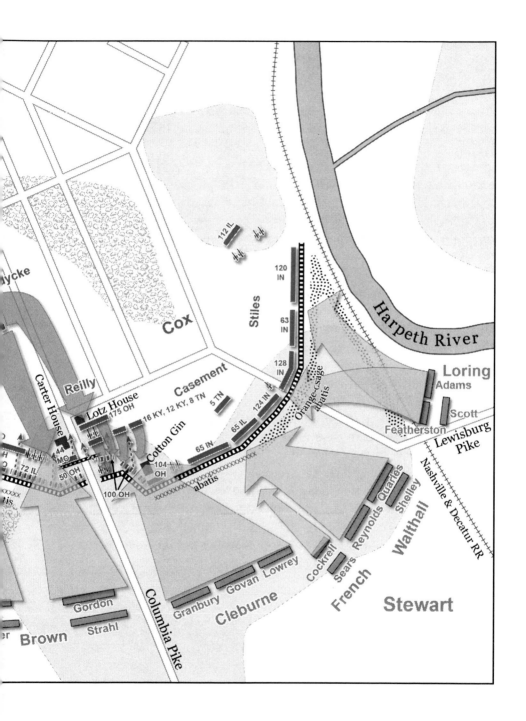

Shortly, another courier rode in with the same request and was given the same answer. "But Hood's whole army is coming!" the man said. "Never mind. Fight them," was Wagner's last reply.[68]

About this time, a battery of field guns that had been out front firing at the oncoming Southerners came down the pike and through the gap in the works, headed for a new position in the rear. Alec Clinton, one of the gunners, shouted to Captain Scofield as he passed, "Old Hell is let loose and coming out there!"[69] If he only knew how true that would prove to be.

Captain John Shellenberger was commanding Company "B" 64th Ohio in Conrad's brigade, and he gives us an idea of how the command to stand and fight was received by the men on the advanced line:

> *The indignation of the men grew almost into a mutiny. The swearing of those gifted in profanity exceeded all their previous efforts.*[70]

By now, some of the thirty-four artillery pieces in and behind the Union line were finding the range and, along with the guns from Fort Granger across the river, were tearing gaps in the advancing Rebel lines. Like the veterans they were, they closed up the ranks and the lines came on. They knew that the worst was yet to come.

Firing could also be heard to the east as Forrest and one of his divisions had crossed the Harpeth River and were dueling with the Federal cavalry. Forrest had been forced by Hood to break up his force, and for the first time, General Wilson and his Yankee riders were getting the best of it. John Schofield's flanks were safe today. John Bell Hood had managed to do what no Federal commander had accomplished during the entire campaign— marginalize and contain "that Devil Forrest." Another of his divisions would see limited action west of Carter's Creek Pike, but by and large, Forrest was hamstrung at Franklin by his own commander.

Chapter 9

DYING LIKE MEN

"If we are to die, let us die like men."
—Major General Patrick Ronayne Cleburne

The Confederate line had started out beautifully dressed across over one mile of open fields, kicking up hundreds of rabbits and dozens of coveys of quail as they went forward, but as they began to close on the Federal advanced line, things began to change. On the right, the Harpeth River was beginning to force some units to the left, and the line was starting to bunch up, with Stewart's units crowding into one another and into Cleburne's division in the center. On the left, William Bate's division, which had the longest distance to go (having to detour around a hill), was falling behind. Meanwhile, more Federal artillerymen were opening up, and the troops in the open were suffering. All this before they had fired a shot. As Cleburne and Brown's men in the center came up to the two Federal brigades out front, it was almost a relief to finally be able to shoot back.

As the Confederate onslaught came on, it was the men of Patrick Cleburne's division plus Gordon's brigade from Brown's division on the west and French's division on the east that collided with Lane and Conrad's men in the Federal advanced line. Even though outnumbered at least two to one, some of the Federals had repeating rifles, and their first couple of salvos staggered the Rebels' first line; they fell back momentarily to regroup. This threw the eastern part of the Confederate line forward as the center hesitated, and most of three divisions now closed on the section of the Federal mainline east of the Columbia Pike, held by only three brigades.

The Union Eastern Flank
4:00 p.m.

With the troops in the center temporarily held up by Wagner's two brigades, the men from A.P. Stewart's corps swept on. On the right, General Loring's two lead brigades under Featherston and Scott had marched through the spacious fields of John McGavock's Carnton Plantation with plenty of room, but as they approached the Federal line, they were being squeezed together by the river on their right, and the artillery fire was murderous. It wasn't until they crossed the last hundred yards that they saw the Osage orange hedge, and it stopped them short. At this point, the Indiana men in Stiles's brigade opened fire, and the Mississippi and Alabama troops were cut to pieces. Some of Featherston's men tried to flank the Federal line by following the railroad that ran next to the river, but small arms fire from the men of the 120th Indiana, canister from two guns of the 4th U.S. Artillery and the three-inch ordinance rifles at Fort Granger across the river turned the railroad cut into a killing ground. The fighting was so close that some of the Indiana men were hit by fire from their own artillery, but Stiles's brigade held firm.

Writing home to his wife a few days later, a young officer in the center of Stiles's line tried to illustrate how much small arms fire his men had laid down. First Lieutenant James S. Pressnall, Company F, 63rd Indiana, wrote that, after the fighting died down, his company captured a Reb in front of their lines who told them that, as men fell all around him, he lay down about fifty yards in front of the lines and hid behind the bodies, so that only an inch or so of his back was still visible. Lieutenant Pressnall then says:

> *I saw myself that eight or ten holes were shot through his close bodied coat just above his shoulders. Three of the shots tore strips of skin of from four to six inches long. His cartridge box straps crossing his back and his belt was both shot entirely off. Also his canteen strap was shot off and his haversack strap only hung by a few threads.*[71]

In the thorny Osage orange hedge and the hellish railroad cut, William Loring's division was stopped cold. He suffered almost 25 percent casualties, including two of his three brigade commanders and nine of his nineteen regimental commanders.

To Loring's left, Edward Walthall's division was faring even worse. The Osage orange thicket had stopped them as well. At first, men tried to make a way through, tearing their hands on the thorns, and officers hacked away with swords, but for the most part, they were shot down as they attacked John Casement's line just west of Lewisburg Pike. Eventually, gaps were found all along the line and many Confederates poured through only to be trapped in the ditch in front of the entrenchments, a place that had its own special horrors. The men of Casement's brigade, some firing Henry repeating rifles, methodically tore Walthall's Tennessee, Alabama and Arkansas regiments apart.

Scores of Confederates spent the next few hours huddling in the ditch along with many more who were wounded or already dead, fighting in the dark with an enemy who was just a few feet away on the other side. One of Walthall's men from the 1st Alabama, Quarles's brigade, remembered it this way, forty-seven years later:

> ...*two lines of men fought with but a pile of dirt between them. In firing, the muzzles of the guns would pass each other, and nine times out of ten, when a man rose to fire, he fell back dead. It is to be remembered that the troops were all in confusion, that there were no organized commands. Officers and soldiers had straggled forward to this point of certain and swift death, and they determined to kill as many as possible in the few minutes they had to live. At frequent intervals the men would rise with the determination to go over and fight it out. Three times Col. Dick Williams rose with the cry, "Follow me!" and three times I seized the tail of his coat and held him back.*[72]

Walthall's division was shattered, suffering over 35 percent casualties. Walthall himself had two horses shot from under him, and eleven brigade and regimental commanders killed or wounded. Farther to the west, the thorn hedge finally thinned out near the cotton gin, creating the only relatively open lane of attack east of Columbia Pike, and two widely separated units were the first to find it.

The first to exploit the gap between the hedge and the pike was Samuel French's Missouri brigade under Brigadier General Francis Marion Cockrell. They were just far enough east not to be delayed much by the Federal advanced line and so had a relatively clear run all the way to the Union mainline. Since most of the other units to his right were still fighting through the hedge, Cockrell's tough-as-nails Missourians may have had the dubious honor of being the first Confederate unit to actually hit the main Union entrenchments. As they closed on the line, almost seven hundred strong, however, they got their own baptism of fire.

When the Missourians were within one hundred yards of the Federal works, two companies on the western end of Colonel John S. Casement's line stood up and fired a torrent of lead with repeating rifles.[73] Adding to the carnage were two twelve-pound Napoleon cannons, firing through openings in the breastworks just in front of the cotton gin. These guns, from Lieutenant Aaron Baldwin's 6th Ohio Light Battery, were absolutely brutal. At close quarters the guns would fire canister, which was a thin case filled with twenty-seven musket balls. In extreme situations, they would load double canister. At Franklin, the fighting around Baldwin's guns became so furious—as the Confederates tried, time after time, to get through and capture the battery—that the artillerymen had other soldiers take off their socks and fill them with rifle bullets. Like the standard canister, these were loaded in front of two and a half pounds of black powder and fired as well.

The destructiveness of a twelve-pound Napoleon firing double canister—or the improvised rounds of socks full of bullets—into men at ranges under fifty yards is almost indescribable. Lieutenant Baldwin himself later commented on the distinctive sound of the firing at Franklin:

> *At every discharge of the guns, there were two sounds—first the explosion and then the crack of the bones.*

At the entrenchments, the artillery crews had to fight to protect the guns as well as serve them. They killed men with axes and picks as they fought to keep the guns in action. At one point, the dead and wounded were piled so high in front of the gun ports that the crews had to drag them out of the way to get the guns back in firing position. In the middle of all this, a teenage Confederate drummer boy came through the smoke carrying a fence rail. He climbed up the embankment and shoved the rail into the muzzle of one of the guns, thinking he could disable it. As the men around him watched in horror, the gun fired and the boy and his drum simply vanished in a pink mist. After the battle, records showed that Baldwin's guns, which could normally manage two rounds per minute, fired at least three hundred rounds at Franklin.[74]

Cockrell's brigade was practically destroyed as a functioning unit. He and four of his regimental commanders were casualties. One of them, Colonel Elijah Gates, came riding off the field with the reins in his teeth, having had both arms broken by gunfire. Going in with 696 men, Cockrell's brigade came out with 277 men uninjured—60 percent losses, the greatest of any Confederate brigade.[75] Behind Cockrell's men came French's other brigade under Brigadier General Claudius Sears, but they fared little better, losing three of their six regimental commanders. Overall losses in French's division exceeded 40 percent. By now, the firing was continuous from the Harpeth River to Carter's cotton gin.

Not long after the Missourians were repulsed, another brigade found a break in the hedges. Brigadier General John Adams's brigade was in Loring's division and had started out on the far eastern flank near the river, but when the units in front of him began to pile up on the Osage orange hedge, Adams brought his men to the left looking for a way around the obstructions, crossing behind Walthall's entire division. Finally, just east of the cotton gin, he brought them through. At this point, something happened that no one who saw it would ever forget.

In spite of being wounded, Adams had somehow managed to stay mounted, and now, as Rebels and Yankees alike watched in stunned admiration, he spurred his horse "Old Charley" out in front of his men and charged alone straight toward the colors of the 65th Illinois. For a few seconds, both sides held their fire. Only when "Old Charley" approached the ditch in front of the entrenchments did the Illinois men shoot the horse and rider down. Adams's body was found outside the fortifications the next morning, and "Old Charley" was found with his front feet on the Federal side of the embankment and his hind feet on the Confederate. Colonel John Casement personally removed Adams's watch and ring and "Old Charley's" saddle and had them returned to Adams's widow. John Adams was part of the famous West Point class of 1846, a classmate of George McClellan, Thomas "Stonewall" Jackson and George Pickett.[76]

From the Harpeth River to Fountain Branch Carter's cotton gin, three divisions of Southern men had done all that was asked of them and more, but the Federal line was just too strong. The Federal casualties were small and the Confederates' near catastrophic, but they never forced a breakthrough. In the center, however, it was a different story.

Chapter 10

INTO THE BELLY OF THE BEAST

"The contending elements of Hell turned loose..."
—regimental history of the 73rd Illinois

The Columbia Pike
4:00 p.m.

George Wagner's two brigades on the advanced line had stopped Pat Cleburne's men along the Columbia Pike momentarily, but the Federals there never really had a chance. They had no support on the flanks, and other Confederate units began to flow around them like water around a rock in the middle of a stream. Soon Cleburne's men, as well as some of John Brown's, were back and stronger this time, and within minutes, Wagner's men would be cut off. One second they were firing at the onrushing Confederates, and the next the Rebels were on them. Nobody knows who broke first—each brigade blamed the other—but it didn't matter. The blue line began to come apart and everyone ran for the rear. The Confederates saw the opportunity immediately and shouted "Run with them into the works!" The retreat became a massive footrace. Men on both sides who were already tired from two days of marching and fighting now faced an eight-hundred-yard sprint to the mainline, and some of them just couldn't make it. Federals were shot from behind or knocked down or captured as they fell exhausted on the road. As they approached the entrenchments, the Confederates were following so closely that it became one huge mob surging up the pike. One Confederate remembered it like this:

> *...as soon as they break to run, our men break after them. They have nearly one-half mile to run to get back to their next line—so here we go right after them and yelling like fury and shooting at them at the same time. Kill some of them before they reach their works, and those that are in the second line of works are not able to shoot us because their own men are in front of us...So here we go, Yanks running for life and we for the fun of it.[77]*

All along the eastern line, the Federals in the trenches and the artillery had a clear field of fire at the attacking Confederates, and they exacted a terrible price, but here in the center, they faced an agonizing dilemma. To fire on the advancing Confederates would mean firing upon hundreds of their own men who were running just ahead of them. The Rebels, of course, knew this perfectly well and pressed their advantage. Wagner's men wanted desperately to get behind the entrenchments, but their comrades in the Federal works couldn't hold their fire forever.

Captain John Shellenberger was one of Wagner's men who made the eight-hundred-yard dash to the mainline, and he finally fell, gasping for breath in the ditch in front of the entrenchments. He managed to look up in time to see what happened when the men in the line could wait no longer. Just over his head from behind the line on both sides of the pike, the better part of four Federal regiments stood up and fired. The storm of lead was enormous—the shock wave alone knocked men off their feet. One of the Confederates who was within one hundred yards of the line when they fired was Brigadier General George Gordon, leading one of John Brown's brigades. Thirty-five years later, he remembered it this way:

> *When they fled, the shout was raised by some of the charging Confederates: "Go into the works with them! Go into the works with them!" This cry was quickly caught up and wildly vociferated from a thousand straining throats as we rushed on after the flying forces we had routed, killing some in our running fire, capturing others who were slow of foot, and sustaining but little loss ourselves until, perhaps, within a hundred paces of their main line and stronghold, when it seemed to me that hell itself had exploded in*

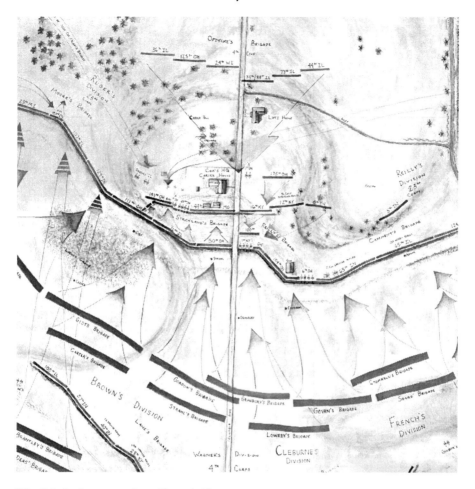

The fight in the center. *Carter House Archives.*

our faces...It yet seems a mystery and a wonder how any of us ever reached the works alive.[78]

Many of them did reach the works alive, but not all. Along the pike, possibly shot down in the first volley, Brigadier General Hiram B. Granbury, leading Cleburne's Texas Brigade, fell, shot through the head. Also into this melee rode Patrick Cleburne himself, urging his men on and determined to make good on his promise to General Hood to take the works or die in the attempt. General Gordon remembered that Cleburne passed so close to him that he had to stop or be trampled by the general's horse. Within one hundred yards or so of the works,

Cleburne's horse was killed, and a second mount, offered by one of his staff, was shot before the general could get aboard, so he went ahead on foot, disappearing into the smoke just east of the pike. His body was discovered the next morning, about fifty yards from the works near the cotton gin, shot through the chest.

The first volley in the center staggered the Confederate front line, but behind them more men kept coming, and within seconds, the mass of the Confederate assault hit the Federal works. The battle in the center now became several fights, all going on at the same time. Cleburne's men, with some of Brown's men mixed in, swarmed through the gap at the pike, and many turned right, coming in behind the lines near the cotton gin. James Riley's men at the works—the 100th and 104th Ohio—suddenly found themselves fighting for their lives along with the artillerymen of the 1st Kentucky Battery who they were supposed to protect. For a few minutes, the area between the pike and the cotton gin was one huge back alley brawl, with hundreds of men fighting with whatever weapon came to hand. At the same time, the men on the west end of John Casement's line, who had just thrown back Cockrell's Missouri brigade, turned to their right and poured a enfilading fire into the flank of Cleburne's men still surging into the center. James Barr, of the 65th Illinois, later said:

> *I was a reenlisted veteran and went through twenty-seven general engagements, but I am sure that Franklin was the hardest fought field I ever stood upon…I never saw men in such a terrible position as Cleburne's Division was in for a few minutes. The wonder is that any of them escaped death or capture.*[79]

Columbia Pike itself was also full of men surging toward the Carter House. In the lead were the survivors of Wagner's advanced line, still running for their lives, and in the middle of this mass of soldiers in blue was General Wagner himself, riding among his men and shouting for them to rally. Despite Wagner's efforts, the mob was bound for the rear and swept him and his horse along with them and out of the fight.

A few of Wagner's men would turn and fight, but most didn't stop until they came to the river. There they came upon both General Schofield and General David Stanley. It was obvious that something had gone wrong at the front, so General Schofield rode to Fort Granger, where he could see most of the field, and General Stanley rode to the front to try and rally the men. For a few minutes, Stanley was in the thick of things, helping to stop some of the fleeing men, until his horse was killed and he was wounded. General Cox then furnished Stanley with another mount and sent him to the rear for medical attention.

Also surging north toward Mr. Carter's house were Ohio and Illinois men from the mainline. While the Confederates to the east of the pike were fighting around the cotton gin, John Brown's men were swarming over the breastworks to the west and into the faces of two Federal regiments. With their left on the pike, the 50th Ohio was immediately overwhelmed, and many of its men began running back toward the retrenchment line behind Mr. Carter's smokehouse, held by the 44th Missouri.

Just to the west of the Ohio men, the 72nd Illinois was also fighting for its life against Rebels coming over the works in waves. As everywhere else, the fight here was unusually close and vicious, with bayonets and clubbed muskets used freely. Captain James Sexton said that he fired his pistol nine times, with the most distant shot being less than twenty feet. Sexton also said that, in the middle of the fight, a Confederate officer came to the top of the parapet and shouted, in "profanely expressive language," for the Yankees to surrender. Without pausing, a private in the ditch below looked up and said, "I guess not," stuck his musket into the Southerner's midsection and blew a hole that Sexton swears was big enough to see light through.[80]

The Chicago men of the 72nd Illinois were trying to hold their own, but when the 50th Ohio broke, they were left unsupported and had to fall back also. When they reformed on the retrenchment line, behind the 44th Missouri and the 183rd Ohio, Captain Sexton found himself the ranking officer of the regiment, all the field grade officers being down.

In what seemed like only moments, Pat Cleburne and John C. Brown's men had forced a breach at least two hundred yards wide in the heart of the Federal line, and hundreds of Confederates led by officers like Colonel Horace Rice of the 29th Tennessee poured through. A few minutes before sundown, it actually seemed possible that John Bell Hood could win his desperate gamble. The Confederates had a chance of cutting the Federal army in two, and the fighting, which had already been as violent and brutal as anybody could remember, would only get worse. The grisly climax of the battle was about to take place in the yard of a nice, quiet grandfather who was at the moment hiding in his own cellar with his family and neighbors.

The Carter House
4:30 p.m.

General Jacob Cox had allowed Fountain Branch Carter and his family to stay in their house on Columbia Pike, largely to keep down the pilfering by the soldiers, as well as because no one really believed that the Southerners would attack the center of the Federal line. Once it became obvious that the Rebels were going to do exactly that, things moved quickly. All Mr. Carter could really do was to move everybody down into the basement and trust that he had built the house well enough to withstand the worst. Earlier in the day, he had taken coils of rope and tried to block the basement windows against stray bullets, and now, as the battle boiled up the hill toward them, the civilians huddled in the center and north rooms of the basement, and the children crowded around their mothers and cried. One of Carter's granddaughters said she remembered that, against Carter's wishes, Federal soldiers also came to the basement to hide and that "Grandpa talked pretty rough to them," but it did no good.[81]

Now just a few minutes before sundown, the brawl around the cotton gin reached its climax as more of Cleburne's men tried to come over the works, and three fresh Federal regiments—men from Kentucky and Tennessee—came forward and pitched into the fight. To the east, A.P. Stewart's men were clinging ferociously to the outer wall and ditch and fighting Israel Stiles and John Casement's men across the entrenchments. West of the gap at the pike, the rest of John Brown's men were coming through the locust grove and fighting hand-to-hand with Colonel Orlando Moore's Federal brigade, and General William Bate's division was finally arriving after marching an extra mile or so. His three brigades were about to go into the fight as well. In the deepening twilight, the entire 1,600-yard Federal front, from the Harpeth River to the Carter's Creek Pike, was alive with fire, and the noise was one continuous roar as almost thirty-five thousand men fought to the death. Just at this time, however, the most critical spot on the battlefield was 100 yards behind the mainline in Fountain Branch Carter's yard.

For the men of the 44th Missouri, holding the retrenchment line behind Carter's office and smokehouse, it must have seemed like a scene out of the "Inferno" of Dante's *Divine Comedy*. First, hundreds of Wagner's men came running past them in panic, and then, as they watched, the mainline, sixty-five yards in front of them, began to cave in, and the men from Ohio and Illinois began to fall back, followed within seconds by a howling mob of Rebels rushing up through Mr. Carter's garden toward them. The 44th's

The Carter House backyard. At the height of the battle, several thousand men fought here. This was the scene of some of the worst hand-to-hand fighting at Franklin. *Author's photo.*

The Carter House farm office (left) and smokehouse (right). After the battle, this small yard was covered with dead and wounded soldiers. *Author's photo.*

position was the last line of defense. If they broke and ran, the next stop was the river; on their first day in combat, the Missouri men braced themselves for the blow and fought like tigers. To the west of Carter's smokehouse, the six artillery pieces tore into the advancing Confederates with round after round of canister until the Rebels swarmed over them and temporarily drove off the crews. The 44th Missouri and men from the reformed 50th Ohio and 72nd Illinois fired volley after volley and cut down the Southern soldiers by the score, but still they came on. One Federal officer in the line later said:

I think I must have fired nearly 200 rounds, and if they did no good, it wasn't my fault. A week after the battle, my right arm was still black from the effect of the kicking gun, although at the time I do not remember to have felt any concussion whatsoever.[82]

Major Arthur MacArthur Jr. Nineteen-year-old MacArthur, future father of General Douglas MacArthur, was wounded three times while leading the 24th Wisconsin regiment into the Carter House yard. *Wisconsin Historical Society image ID#4502.*

Within minutes of the Confederate breakthrough, the Carter House yard and vegetable garden were covered with soldiers, both blue and gray, and more were on the way. Colonel Emerson Opdycke, after his shouting match with General Wagner, had put his six regiments in a field about two hundred yards north of the Carter House. As the Confederates formed up and marched on the advanced line, General Cox had sent a staff officer to Opdycke telling him to be ready since he and his men were now the reserves for the center of the line. When the survivors of Conrad's and Lane's brigades came streaming up the pike and the heavy firing began at the Carter house, Opdycke and his men needed no further orders. Even before Opdycke could issue the command, his regiments began moving up both sides of Columbia Pike on their own, and another 1,500 men entered the swirling slaughterhouse that had its vortex in the Carter yard and spread out for a couple hundred yards east and west.

Opdycke's brigade waded into the fight with some semblance of organization, but once there it quickly became a free-for-all. Nineteen-year-old Major Arthur MacArthur Jr. was wounded three times leading the 24th Wisconsin onto Mr. Carter's property, but survived to become the father of Douglas MacArthur who, like his father, would one day be awarded the Medal of Honor. Some men felt fear while others felt a terrible sort of excitement. A young Union soldier said:

> *I had never experienced this exaltation before, when all prudence is thrust aside. But this time and this time only, had I known the next moment would annihilate me, I would not have flinched a particle.*[83]

Sam Watkins, a young Confederate from Maury County, Tennessee, just thirty miles away, was at that moment fighting southwest of the Carter yard with the 1st Tennessee Infantry, and he simply said:

> *I had made up my mind to die—felt glorious!*[84]

Just before sundown, there were at least five thousand men in Mr. Carter's yard. The fighting there was hand-to-hand and desperate almost beyond belief, and the noise was deafening. One of the children in the basement later said that it was so loud that she couldn't hear herself scream. Even though these were modern nineteenth-century armies, a Roman legionnaire or a Greek hoplite would have felt at home in Mr. Carter's yard or around his cotton gin, fighting hand-to-hand, one man's strength against another's. Men killed and maimed one another with every conceivable weapon, and no one who was there ever forgot it. The regimental history of the 73rd Illinois put it this way:

> *The contending elements of Hell turned loose would seem almost as a Methodist love feast compared to the pandemonium that reigned there for the space of ten or twenty minutes. The scenes that we witnessed during that short space of time were so indelibly stamped upon the minds of the participants that even a long life…will not suffice to erase or even dim them.*[85]

Mercifully, such a fight can't last long, and shortly the weight of the Federal reinforcements began to tell, and the Confederates begin to give ground. By sundown, their breakthrough in the center was contained. The Southerners had been cleared from behind the lines at the cotton gin and pushed over the works into the ditch on the far side. The Confederates in the Carter yard fell back across the mainline of works in their area, while the Federals held the line behind the Carter office and smokehouse. The sixty-five yards in between became a no man's land on which nothing could live in the firing that came in from four directions.

West of the original gap, the rest of Brown's division fought over the entrenchments, and William Bate's men did the same—the better part of two Confederate divisions attacking the position held by one reinforced Federal brigade. West of the Carter's Creek Pike, one brigade of Bate's division and some dismounted cavalry under General James Chalmers made a few attacks on General Nathan Kimball's line but were easily thrown back.

Nobody could say that Pat Cleburne hadn't made good on his pledge to General Hood. Cleburne himself and one of his brigade commanders, Hiram Granbury, lay dead on the field and thirteen of his regimental commanders were killed, wounded or captured. What remained of one of the best and proudest division in the Army of Tennessee was either huddled in the ditch outside the works near the cotton gin, were wounded, dead or prisoners or had somehow managed to withdraw. It's estimated that Cleburne's division suffered over 50 percent casualties.

Twenty-four hours ago, John C. Brown had halted his entire division at the appearance of a few hundred Yankees on his flank. Today, he held nothing back. His brigade under George Gordon hit the center with Cleburne's men, and General Gordon was captured near the cotton gin.

Another of Brown's brigade commanders, General States Rights Gist of South Carolina, went into the battle mounted on his horse "Joe" over the objection of his servant, "Uncle Wiley" Howard. "Marse States, you ain't got no business riding Joe," Howard told him. "Joe ain't got no sense when the bullets come around." "He'll have to get used to the bullets," General Gist had replied. As Uncle Wiley watched, Gist led his men through the locust grove, and just as he had feared, Joe was soon wounded and Gist had to dismount from the plunging animal. The last time Uncle Wiley saw his master, General Gist was leading his men on foot past a large maple tree. Within minutes, Gist would be hit in the leg and the right lung, and the next time his servant saw him, Gist was lying dead in a field hospital.[86] The rest of Gist's brigade fought

Colonel Orlando Moore's 111th Illinois and 129th Indiana regiments tooth and nail across the entrenchments.

Brown's two other brigades under Otho Strahl and John C. Carter followed immediately. General Strahl, along with many of his men, was trapped in the ditch along the outside wall of the works just south of the Carter House. As it happened, the Federal line on the east side of the pike was far enough advanced that the Yankees there could face to their right and actually fire directly down the outside wall to the west of the pike, and they slaughtered Strahl's men there like sheep in a pen. General Strahl was wounded at the works, and then, as he was being carried to the rear, he and all his staff were shot down and killed.

Farther west, General John C. Carter was wounded leading his men through the locust grove. Carter would linger for ten days before his wounds proved fatal. In the middle of all this, General Brown himself was seriously wounded and had to be taken off the field. His division lost its commander, all four brigade commanders, five regimental commanders and suffered about 31 percent losses overall.[87]

By comparison, William Bate's losses were more modest—about 15 percent—but one of his casualties was especially tragic. In one of Bate's brigades, commanded by Brigadier General Thomas Benton Smith, a twenty-four-year-old captain served as the general's aide. Even though it wasn't his primary duty, the young

Captain Theodrick (Tod) Carter, aide to Brigadier General Thomas B. Smith. Tod Carter was the middle son of Fountain Branch Carter, owner of the Carter House. Tod was wounded near his father's vegetable garden and found by his family after the battle. He died of his wounds the next day in the house where he was born twenty-four years earlier. *Carter House Archives.*

captain insisted on going to the front. While the opposing commanders had once been West Point roommates, and several other senior commanders on both sides were friends, no one else had a personal stake at Franklin like the general's aide. The young captain's name was Theodrick Carter, known to his friends and family as "Tod," and he had been born and raised in the brick house on the small hill just a few hundred yards away. As he went forward, his father, his elder brother, four sisters, a sister-in-law and his nine nieces and nephews waited in the basement for the fighting to stop. During the assault, Tod and his favorite horse, "Rosencrantz," were shot down near the works, and along with many other men, he lay on the field seriously wounded for most of the night.

The sun had finally gone down, but the darkness only served to make the flashes of gunfire brighter as thousands of men continued to fight across the Federal works, and incredibly, the Rebels weren't finished. Just as the battle was beginning, General Steven D. Lee arrived from Spring Hill ahead of his corps and asked where he was needed. From two miles away, about all General Hood could see was smoke and flames, so he told General Lee to bring up his first division and confer with General Frank Cheatham, who was nearer the front. It was almost 5:00 p.m. before Lee and Cheatham met, and Cheatham had little more solid information than General Hood. Cheatham simply pointed to the north and said:

> *Yonder line of fire at the breastworks is where you are needed and wanted at once. There is the place your division is to go and the sooner you put your men in, the better, as the slaughter has been terrible with my brave men.*

When General Lee asked at least for a guide to lead his men through the darkness to their attack positions, Cheatham said that he had no one left to send since all his staff were either dead or already gone to the front.[88]

Major General Ed Johnson commanded the division that Lee was adding to the fight, and he had four brigades with about 2,700 men. By the time Johnson's men were in position, it was 7:00 p.m., two hours after sundown. Cheatham had warned General Johnson to be careful about his men's aim, since there were already hundreds of his men along the outside of the works who they might kill as readily as Yankees. How they were supposed to do this in the dark wasn't explained. As they groped through the darkness to find the Federal entrenchments, some of the men on each end of the line carried torches, which was a great help to the Northern men in aiming their volleys.

Ed Johnson and his men went in with as much valor as any of the Southern soldiers, and they were handled every bit as roughly as the men who attacked in daylight. Johnson's division made no more permanent dent in the Federal line than had their comrades before them. In the end, they only added to the mass of suffering and dying men, losing nine brigade and regimental commanders. The ghastly struggle between thousands of soldiers, groping in the dark for one another across a few feet of dirt wall or simply huddling in the increasingly cold night all over the battlefield, went on for another two hours before the fighting finally died away out of sheer exhaustion on both sides sometime after 9:00 p.m.

Perversely, the end of the firing only brought fresh horrors. Now that the guns were silent, all along the front for almost one mile, every man could hear the sounds of thousands of wounded and dying men out there in the cold, clear night—cursing, screaming, praying, begging for water, calling for their mothers or simply moaning as they lay freezing and bleeding in the dark. For many of those wounded men, it was truly a night where some of the living envied the dead. For the men on the battlefield lucky enough to be unhurt, the sounds were like a waking nightmare.

Many of the Northern soldiers who had inflicted so much damage on the Rebel army were deeply affected by what they heard from in front of their lines after the battle died down. On the eastern end of the Federal line, an officer of the 63rd Indiana recalls what he and his men experienced:

> *Amid the hundreds of dead and wounded Confederates who lay thickly scattered over the field in our front...there was one lying in front of my company, only a few feet distant crying "Mother...you were right, you'll never see your boy again. I'm dying out here in the dark...I'm bleeding to death." The boy's voice became gradually weaker and weaker until we heard it no more...One of the company's new recruits, a mere boy in years, was crying as though his heart was broken. He too was the only son of a widowed mother.*[89]

John Bell Hood's army was shattered, even though he wouldn't know the full extent of the disaster until the next morning. Even so, he wasn't ready to quit. Just as at Spring Hill the day before, Hood believed that the Yankees would still be there in the morning, and he was committed to a fight to the finish. General S.D. Lee was told to ready his remaining two divisions to renew the attack and to position all the artillery for a massive bombardment to begin at 7:00 a.m. General Stewart and General Cheatham both said that he couldn't count on much help from their decimated units, but Hood was determined to go ahead anyway. Mercifully, it wouldn't be necessary. General John Schofield had no desire to press his luck any further. General Jacob Cox's defense had been all he could have asked for, his wagon trains were all across the river and now it was time to go.[90] By midnight, the Federal infantry was filing out of the works and crossing the Harpeth River, and within a few hours, even their pickets would be gone, leaving only the dead and wounded who couldn't be moved.[91]

Finally, the fighting was over, and all that was left were the sounds of thousands of men lying wounded, thirsty and freezing on the field—sounds that would haunt all who heard them for the rest of their days. The heart had been ripped out of the Southern army. As the brigade on the left end of the Federal line was preparing to pull out, one of Colonel Israel Stiles's officers said, "We ought to remain here and wipe hell out of them." Stiles simply replied, "There's no hell left in them. Don't you hear them praying?"[92]

Chapter 11

THE MORNING AFTER

"God forgive me for ever wishing to see or hear a battle."
—*Mrs. Carrie Snyder, civilian visitor in Franklin*

By dawn on December 1, all of the Federal forces were across the Harpeth River on their way to Nashville, but before they left, many of the Northern men had gone across the entrenchments to see what they could of the field in the darkness. One of them was Captain John Shellenberger of the 64th Ohio, who went out looking for some of his men:

> *I went to a gun of the 6th Ohio battery, posted a short distance east of the cotton gin, to get over…in the dim starlight. The mangled bodies of the dead rebels were piled up as high as the mouth of the embrasure and the gunners said that repeatedly when the lanyard was pulled the embrasure was filled with men crowding forward to get in, who were literally blown from the mouth of the cannon. Only one rebel got past the muzzle of the gun and one of the gunners snatched up a pick…and killed him with that.*
>
> *While I was cautiously making my way around one side of that mangled heap of humanity, a wounded man lying at the bottom, with head and shoulders protruding, begged me, for the love of Christ, to pull the dead bodies off him. The ditch was piled promiscuously with the dead and badly wounded and heads, arms and legs were sticking out in almost every conceivable manner. The ground near the ditch was filled with the moans of the wounded and the pleadings of some…for water and for help were heartrending.*[93]

Across the pike, opposite the locust grove, Colonel Issac Sherwood of the 111th Ohio Infantry did his own survey before pulling his regiment out of the works, where they had fought the men of States Rights Gist and John C. Carter's brigades to a standstill:

> *I stood on the parapet just before midnight and saw all that could be seen. I saw and heard all that my eyes could see, or my rent soul contemplate in such an awful environment. It was a spectacle to chill the stoutest heart…The wounded, shivering in the chilled November air; the heartrending cries of the desperately wounded and the prayers of the dying filled me with an anguish that no language can describe. From that hour, I have hated war.*[94]

The Federal troops left their places as quietly as possible and crossed the river with little trouble. One unit, however, had a nasty incident. First Lieutenant James S. Pressnall, commanding Company "F" of the 63rd Indiana, was marching his company through town to the footbridge when a woman ran out of a house along the street, screaming over and over, "The yanks are retreating!" As an old man, Pressnall still remembered the event vividly:

> *At once, amidst her wild screaming, one of my company, without orders from me or anyone, stepped quickly to her and, with the muzzle of his gun within two or three feet of her body, shot her through the heart, returning instantly to his place in the ranks. A very distressing incident—but such is war.*

Lieutenant Pressnall's company and regiment were part of the rear guard of the Federal Army on its march to Nashville, but having been marching, digging or fighting for the last forty-eight hours, they like most of the Federal men were hard-pressed to put one foot in front of the other:

> *In the night march from Franklin to Nashville, our regiment, by reason of its worn down condition and loss of sleep, were entirely unfitted to properly perform the duties assigned it as rear guard of our retreating army. We had all we could do to take care of ourselves. With utmost care taken to keep our men on their feet and in line of march, we lost three during the night, who were picked up by the advancing enemy.*[95]

The Morning After

With the Yankees gone, Confederates began to move into Franklin before dawn, and one of the early visitors called at Fountain Branch Carter's house. The family had come up from the cellar not long before, and Brigadier General Thomas Benton Smith, Tod Carter's commander, found eight-year-old Alice McPhail on the back porch. "Missie, is this where Squire Carter lives?" he asked. When told that it was, he said, "Tell him Captain Carter is severely wounded on the field and I will show him about where to find him." Fountain Branch Carter and his daughters lit lanterns and followed General Smith on foot out past his smokehouse, across his garden and to the Federal works, where his son and his horse were found. Captain Tod Carter was carried unconscious back to the house, where Dr. Deering Roberts removed a ball from his forehead and dressed eight other wounds. Tod's eleven-year-old niece, Lena Carter, held the lantern over the operating table in the parlor during her uncle's surgery. He was then carried to a bedroom, where his sisters did what they could for him, but he never regained consciousness and died the next day, in the same house where he was born.

Many strange stories came out of the Civil War, but few soldiers can claim to have served for over three years, only to fight their final battle in their father's garden and die of their wounds in their own bed. Unlike most other

The Carter House, circa 1890. *Carter House Archives.*

young men who died at Franklin, Tod Carter was given a funeral in his home and was buried in the local family plot.[96]

In the predawn hours, other Southern men began to move across the battlefield, some simply to see what had happened and others searching for friends who were missing. One of these was John McQuaide. He was serving in A.P. Stewart's artillery and had been preparing for the dawn bombardment when orders came down cancelling it. He then rode forward to see the situation for himself, and within fifty or sixty yards of the entrenchments near the cotton gin, he found the body of General Patrick Cleburne. He had been shot once through the chest, and his boots and other valuables had been stolen in the night.

Some distance to the east, McQuaide saw an ambulance wagon and went to report General Cleburne's whereabouts. There he found Chaplin Thomas Markham of Featherston's Brigade and two helpers loading the body of General John Adams into the wagon. Together they went to where General Cleburne lay and loaded his body alongside General Adams, taking them both to Carnton, the home of John McGavock, which had become the hospital for General A.P. Stewart's corps. Adams and Cleburne were laid out on Carnton's back porch, where they would be joined later by the bodies of Hiram Granbury and Otho Strahl as they were brought in.[97]

Carnton Plantation, home of John and Carrie McGavock. Before the battle, General Forrest used this back porch as an observation post. The next morning, the bodies of Confederate generals John Adams, Patrick Cleburne, Hiram Granbury and Otho Strahl were laid out here. Carnton served as the hospital for Lieutenant General A.P. Stewart's corps. *Author's photo.*

The Morning After

Among the Confederates to ride into Franklin before sunrise was Frank Cheatham, whose men had broken the center of the Federal line and suffered so terribly in the process. A soldier from the 19th Tennessee said later that he saw Cheatham along the pike, walking among his fallen soldiers with a torch. The hard-fighting, hard-drinking, often-profane veteran of many terrible battles wept, and "great big tears ran down his cheeks, as he looked into the faces of dead friends and listening to the cries of hundreds of his wounded men"[98] Cheatham himself, almost twenty years later, remembered it this way:

> *Just at daybreak, I rode upon the field, and such a sight I never saw and can never expect to see again. The dead were piled up like stacks of wheat or scattered about like sheaves of grain. You could have walked all over the field upon dead bodies without stepping upon the ground...Almost under your eye, nearly all the dead, wounded and dying lay. In front of the Carter house, the bodies lay in heaps, and to the right of it, a locust thicket had been mowed off by bullets, as if by a scythe. It was a wonder that any man escaped alive...I never saw anything like that field, and never want to again.*[99]

Now that the fighting was over, the attention turned to caring for the wounded and the grim task of burying the dead. Dr. Deering Roberts, of the 20th Tennessee, who had treated Tod Carter at his father's house, continued downtown. Roberts's primary duty was to set up facilities for the care of casualties from General William Bate's division, and he selected several buildings in the town and put men to work preparing them for the wounded by building crude bunks and spreading fresh straw on the floors.

Southeast of town, wounded men were streaming into Carnton, the McGavock plantation house, and Carrie McGavock, the lady of the house, welcomed all comers as best she could. Soon, except for one small room kept for the family, every bed and every foot of floor space was taken by injured and dying men, with more ambulances and walking wounded arriving all the time. The house was soon full, and the patients were put on the porches and finally filled the yard and outbuildings. The doctors were overwhelmed, and many of the wounded had to wait for hours while the more serious were treated. The surgeons worked nonstop all day, and amputated limbs were stacked in piles outside the makeshift operating rooms.

Carrie McGavock and her family moved among the maimed and dying men, giving what comfort they could—a cup of tea, a bite to eat, writing down

Carrie McGavock, "the Angel of Carnton." *Historic Carnton Plantation.*

a final message to a loved one or just a kind word. As she moved through the house, the hem of her dress became soaked in blood, and when bandages ran out, Carrie offered her table linen and then her bedding, her husband's shirts and finally her own underclothes. To the hundreds of broken and tortured souls who passed through her house after the battle, Carrie McGavock became known as "the Angel of Carnton."

Farther north at the Carter House, the same kind of scene was playing out. Not as large as Carnton, the Carter House served more as a surgical station, to which the casualties would be brought and evaluated and at which amputations or other surgical procedures were performed. The men would then be moved down into town to be cared for in the hospitals being set up in almost every major building. By evening, a pile of amputated limbs over six feet high had collected outside the window next to the operating table in the parlor, and all the carpets in the house were soaked with blood. Both of these houses have many traces of blood still detectable after fourteen decades.

Along with the Confederate soldiers, some townspeople began to come out and view the scene. Hardin Figuers, a local teenager, remembered walking up the Columbia Pike toward the Federal line:

> *Right in front of the Carter House, on the margin of the pike, there was a locust tree about five inches in diameter…A Yankee soldier standing behind this tree was shot through the head. His left shoulder was against the tree, his head had dropped to his bosom, his gun in his left hand had kept him from falling on the left side, and his heavy iron ramrod in his*

right hand had supported him on that side, and there he was standing in that position, dead.[100]

Young Figuers walked on past the Carter House down to the Federal mainline and got his first look at the larger battlefield:

From Lewisburg Pike on the east, along in front of and just south of the Federal breastworks as far as the Columbia Pike and west of the Pike as far as the locust thicket, the dead and wounded were so thick upon the ground that it might be said without exaggeration that one could walk upon the dead and never touch the ground.

I remember seeing one poor fellow, sitting up and leaning back against something, whose lower jaw had been cut off by a grape shot, and his tongue and under lip were hanging down on his breast. I knelt down and ask if I could do anything for him. He had a little piece of pencil and an envelope... he wrote: "No. John B. Hood will be in New York before three weeks."[101]

Brave words indeed, but it's doubtful that the Army of Tennessee's commander himself was quite so optimistic.

Just about this time, General John Bell Hood rode into town with some of his staff to see the results of the battle firsthand. Like General Frank Cheatham before him, he paused on the Columbia Pike where it passed through the Federal line and tried to take in the magnitude of the carnage. One soldier who saw Hood as he surveyed the scene said that "[f]or a considerable time he sat on his horse and wept like a child." He then rode on into town and dismounted in the yard of Mrs. William Sykes. There he sat in a chair and tried to decide what the army would do now.[102] Little Alice McPhail remembered seeing him there:

I remember going with Aunt Sallie over to Mrs. Sykes'...and we saw a man sitting in a chair in the yard. He looked so sad, and Grandpa told me it was Gen. Hood.

Hardin Figuers remembered seeing him too:

I distinctly remember seeing Gen. Hood riding down through the streets of Franklin with his wooden leg and his long, tawny mustache and whiskers. I...was much disappointed.[103]

In spite of the shock, the Army of Tennessee began to pull itself together, and by mid-morning, it was going about the grisly work of burying the dead and tending the wounded. Two young men who were in those burial details give some idea what it was like. Washington Ives, of the 4th Florida Infantry, said:

> *I saw at 10:00 am* [twelve hours after the end of the fighting] *human blood three inches deep in the main line and running like water. It was impossible to bury all our dead in one day.*

W.G. Bell, of Company "G", 14th Mississippi Infantry, summed it up as well as anyone:

> *I helped bury the dead at Franklin, and I think I could have walked all over the battlefield on dead men. There is no language that could picture that battle, and there is of little use for me to try.*[104]

More civilians were now coming out from town to see the battlefield and to help with the wounded. One was a young lady named Carrie Snyder who was visiting in town. Carrie's husband was a railroad engineer, and she was a little worried when the Confederate army came to town because she was known to be a Union sympathizer. Even so, she was excited at first because she had always wanted to witness a battle. When artillery shells began to fly past the house at which she was staying, however, Carrie ran to the cellar with the rest, where they stayed most of the night. Now that morning had come, Carrie was determined to see the battlefield for herself, even though the Federal army had marched away and left her in Confederate-occupied territory. What she saw did not change her Union sympathy, but it changed her attitude about battle. Later she wrote:

> *God forgive me for ever wanting to see or hear a battle!…You had to look twice as you picked your way among the bodies to see which were dead and which were alive and often a dead man would be lying partly on a live one, or the reverse—and the groans, the sickening smell of blood!…I noticed while wandering along the earthworks that all or nearly all of the Union soldiers were shot in the foreheads…In front, the ground was covered with bodies and pools of blood…The cotton in the old cotton gin was shot out all over the ground…*
> *Our* [Union] *soldiers had been stripped of everything but their shirts and drawers, but the Confederate soldiers could not be blamed much for that,*

for they were half clothed, half barefoot, and many of them bareheaded, but I saw one thing I thought contemptible. A fine looking Union soldier had been stripped of all but his shirt and drawers. He was lying off by himself at the roadside near the depot. He was apparently an officer. His shirt was fine flannel. "H'yar," says a big Confederate, calling to some of his men. "H'yar's a mighty fine shut [sic] on this ere dead yank," giving him a kick. I thought it was bad enough to strip him of hat, coat, pants, boots and socks; they might at least give him a single garment to bury him in.[105]

While the wounded were being tended and hospitals being set up in town, the burial details worked along the mainline and in Mr. Carter's fields. In many places, the outside ditch was filled with bodies, and the dirt from the earthworks was simply pulled down onto them. In the fields, trenches were dug two and a half feet deep and wide enough for two bodies, side by side. A blanket or cloth was placed over their faces and the dirt shoveled back on. When it was possible to identify a body, a wooden plank would be placed with the name and unit. For the most part, the Federal dead were buried last, thrown into the trenches at the mainline and covered there.[106]

All of the dead weren't at the mainline, however. One hundred yards behind the lines on the Columbia Pike, Fountain Branch Carter's property was a shambles. His house, farm office, smokehouse and kitchen were riddled with small arms fire. They still stand today, the most battle-damaged Civil War buildings still in existence. The southern end of the main house was so badly damaged that it had to be refaced with new brick. Moscow Carter counted fifty-seven dead soldiers in the small yard just off his back porch and many more in his front yard—literally on his doorstep. Eighteen years later, he remembered what it was like trying to clean up after the battle:

In this yard and in that garden, I could walk from fence to fence on bodies, mostly those of Confederates. In trying to clear up, I scraped together a half bushel of brains right around the house, and the whole place was dyed in blood. Nothing in the shape of horse, mule, jack nor jenny was left in this neighborhood. In fact, I remember it was not until Christmas, twenty-five days afterwards, that I was enabled to borrow a yoke of oxen, and I spent the whole of that Christmas Day hauling seventeen dead horses from this yard.[107]

Down in town, the hospitals were getting organized and the citizens were pitching in. All of the major structures were put into service, and

Moscow B. Carter, Fountain Branch Carter's eldest son. A paroled Confederate officer, Moscow and his children were part of the group in his father's basement. It later fell to Moscow to clean up the property after the battle was over and the armies had left. *Carter House Archives.*

many of the local ladies took responsibility for the wounded in their homes or in a church or other building. Hardin Figuers's mother, Bethenia Figuers, had wounded in her house and was also in charge of the men at the Episcopal church. Before it was over, forty-four structures in town became hospitals.

Young Hardin spent the next few days tending the wounded himself, as well as going out into the countryside with an old dump cart searching for food to feed the men:

> *We would take a large wash kettle, about twenty gallons, and make it full of soup with plenty of red pepper. For this soup, I brought in…Irish potatoes, cabbage, dried beans, and turnips, and…we used any kind of meat obtainable. The soldiers thought this was great diet, in fact the best they had had for more than a year.*

The Morning After

The day of the battle had been pleasant, an Indian summer day, but then it started to rain, and winter came to middle Tennessee. Again, Hardin Figuers remembered:

> *The rain on the third day after the battle turned into a snow, and during the next eighteen days that the Confederates occupied the town, it was the most terrible spell of weather I ever knew. There were snow, sleet, and ice continually, with the thermometer down to zero. Food got scarcer and scarcer every day.*[108]

At Franklin at least, the wounded had shelter from the inclement weather. By that Saturday, most of what was left of the Army of Tennessee had marched north eighteen miles or so to Nashville and had to endure the same weather while living in tents or simply out in the open in holes dug in the ground. Any Confederate soldier who had shoes on his feet, a coat or a blanket against the cold or a tent to shield him from the sleet and snow considered himself lucky. Many were not so fortunate. Meanwhile, a Federal army almost three times their number waited snug behind their fortifications for the orders to go out and attack.

For the moment, the fighting was over in Franklin. The armies were now facing each other at Nashville. What was left at the town on the Harpeth River was a field full of graves and a community of wounded men who numbered five or six times the civilian population who had to care for, feed and house them.

Chapter 12

THE DEATH OF HOOD'S ARMY

"You can talk about your Beauregard and sing of General Lee, but the gallant Hood of Texas played hell in Tennessee."
—song reportedly sung to the tune of "Yellow Rose of Texas" by the remnants of the Army of Tennessee as they retreated into northern Mississippi

While the burial parties were being organized at Franklin on December 1, General Nathan Bedford Forrest's riders were already moving north up Wilson Pike, paralleling Schofield's army on its eastern flank. S.D. Lee's corps would soon follow, and by December 3, the bulk of the Confederate army was strung out on an east–west line on the south edge of Nashville, except for Forrest's cavalry and William Bate's infantry division, which had been diverted to reduce the Federal garrison at Murfreesboro.

Perhaps nothing says more about the desperate situation of the Confederate army or of its commander's grasp of reality than this: John Bell Hood considered marching his twenty thousand or so remaining effective troops farther north in the dead of winter and laying siege to one of the most heavily fortified cities on the continent, held by a Federal army almost three times his size, to be his best remaining option. After the war, with the benefit of some years of hindsight, Hood wrote in his memoirs that the men's morale could not stand a retreat. He was also hoping for reinforcements from Trans-Mississippi, but there is no evidence that he had ever been led to expect any such thing from Richmond. Knowing that a withdrawal south from Franklin, although the most rational thing to do, would be seen as a defeat, it may well be that this was simply the only other thing he could think of to do.

Whatever his rationale, his army now sat outside of Nashville, cold and hungry and watching the well-fed Yankees in their heated huts, for two weeks. General George Thomas was under intense pressure from Washington to attack and destroy Hood's army and was almost relieved of command for his delay, but on December 15 he came out of his fortifications and by the afternoon of the next day, Hood's army had been broken and was in headlong retreat. Few of his units retained any organization, and they were all headed back south down the pike. By December 18, the Federals had reoccupied Franklin, with all its hospitals. Even at that time, after many of the wounded had been moved or the walking wounded sent home to recuperate with relatives, Federal troops still reported capturing 3,800 wounded men and 702 other prisoners and finding "1,750 buried on the field." This would make the official Confederate casualties at Franklin 6,252, but the real number could have easily exceeded 7,000. Particularly hard hit at Franklin were Confederate general and field grade officers. Along with 53 regimental officers, 15 generals were casualties, effectively "gutting" the command structure of several infantry divisions. Total official Federal losses at Franklin were 2,326.[109]

Only a heroic rear guard action south of the Duck River, led by Forrest with about 3,000 of his cavalry and 1,600 infantry under General Edward C. Walthall, saved Hood's army from annihilation as Thomas's troops pressed them all the way to the Tennessee River. By December 27, Hood had managed to get what was left across to the south side of the river and relative safety. Also, because of the campaign, a swath of middle Tennessee from Nashville to the Alabama line had been picked clean by the soldiers of both armies, and hundreds of civilians now faced the winter hungry and destitute.

A passage from General Thomas J. Wood's after-action report gives a picture of the once proud Army of Tennessee as 1865 opened. Addressed to General George Thomas, it reads in part:

> *Feel confident that Hood has not taken across the Tennessee River more than half the men he brought across it; that no more than half of those taken out were armed; that he lost three fourths of his artillery and, that for rout, demoralization, even disintegration, the condition of his command is without parallel in this war.*[110]

For all practical purposes, the Confederate Army of Tennessee had ceased to exist as a viable military force. The effects of Hood's campaign in terms of human suffering, while appalling, are somewhat subjective, but the cold statistics are not. The most recent and probably the best figures are provided by historian Eric Jacobson who after sifting through the available records concludes that Hood, having brought about 33,000 armed men into middle Tennessee, must have lost at least 15,952 of them during the thirty-six-day campaign. Under Hood, the Army of Tennessee lost almost half its effective force, along with much of its arms and equipment, and wound up back where it started. By any measure, Hood's conduct of the Tennessee Campaign was an unmitigated disaster.[111]

To continue to list statistics can become tedious, but to understand the scope of what happened at Franklin, a little perspective can be helpful. Franklin was probably the deadliest battle of the Civil War for Confederate soldiers, when the men killed are viewed as a percentage of total casualties. For most major battles, that percentage is around 15 percent or less. At Gettysburg, the largest battle ever fought in the Western Hemisphere, the ratio rises to 20 percent. At Franklin, that same ratio exceeds 25 percent.

Rarely was there a time or place in the war that exceeded the intensity, violence, fact-to-face combat and sheer brutality of that first hour at Franklin. Historians estimate that as many as 70 to 80 percent of the casualties at Franklin may have been inflicted during that time. The Civil War brought a level of carnage to America that remains unmatched, before or since. The combat casualties in one afternoon at Franklin exceeded the combat dead and wounded of either the War of 1812 or the twenty-month-long Mexican-American War, which provided the training ground for most of the senior Civil War commanders on both sides.

For a modern comparison, consider that on D-Day, the Allies had about 155,000 men engaged against a modern German army with pre-sighted artillery and automatic weapons. That force—over four times more men—suffered roughly the same number of casualties on the first day of the invasion as the armies at Franklin, using nineteenth-century weapons, inflicted on one another in five hours.

About the same number of Americans assaulted Omaha Beach as fought at Franklin, but only suffered two to three thousand casualties. Although the men still living who were actually there would probably deny it, statistically it was almost three times safer to be in a landing craft approaching Omaha Beach on June 6, 1944, than it was charging the Federal mainline at Franklin on November 30, 1864.

CONFEDERATE GENERAL OFFICERS KILLED
AT FRANKLIN

Above, left: Major General Patrick Royanne Cleburne, division commander under Frank Cheatham. Under a cloud from Spring Hill, Cleburne promised to take the Union works or die in the attempt. He was killed in front of the cotton gin. Cleburne was the highest-ranking officer killed at Franklin. *Library of Congress.*

Above, right: Brigadier General John Adams, brigade commander under William Loring. Killed leading his men against the Union line east of the cotton gin, Adams and his horse "Old Charley" were shot down as they tried to leap the Union works held by the 65th Illinois. *Tennessee State Library and Archives.*

Opposite above, left: Brigadier General Hiram Bronson Granbury, brigade commander under Pat Cleburne. Granbury was killed on the Columbia Pike leading Cleburne's Texas Brigade during the first assault in the center. Granbury may have been the first general killed at Franklin. *Carter House Archives.*

Opposite above, right: Brigadier General Otho French Strahl, brigade commander under John C. Brown. Strahl and many of his men were trapped in the outer ditch in front of the Union works. He was wounded at the works and then killed as he was being carried to the rear. *Tennessee Historical Society.*

Opposite below, left: Brigadier General John C. Carter, brigade commander under John C. Brown. Carter was mortally wounded leading his troops against the Union works near the locust grove. Carter was taken to a nearby house, where he lingered for ten days before his wound proved fatal. *Tennessee State Library and Archives.*

Opposite below, right: Brigadier General States Rights Gist, brigade commander under John C. Brown. Gist led his men through the locust grove, where he was wounded twice. He died later that night at an aid station. *Carter House Archives.*

Given our advantage of almost a century and a half of hindsight, speculation about how Civil War battles might have turned out differently is almost irresistible. Recent authors have, in fact, used that method to sell a great number of books of "alternate history." For the Battle of Franklin, the temptation is greater than most. Neither side wanted to fight at Franklin, but the Confederates had to attack before sundown or let the Federal army escape again—this time to Nashville. Because of the delay with the bridge, the Federals had to fight with their backs to the river. The attack was to a great extent an act of desperation by the Confederates, and the Federals had no easy line of retreat, so both sides were committed by their circumstances to fight to the bitter end. From the Federal side, Captain J.A. Sexton of the 72nd Illinois put it this way:

> *Franklin was a private soldier's battle, the sum of its strategy being to hold and occupy the few square feet which the soldiers stood to the last.*[112]

It would be no exaggeration to say that the whole battle turned on the lack of a bridge. The obvious question, then, is what would have happened if the bridging pontoons had been delivered on time. If Schofield had been able to move most of his wagons over the river by noon instead of 3:00 p.m., he could have then withdrawn his infantry in plenty of time to face Hood's army with the Harpeth River between them. Then there would have been no grand assault, and after dark, the Federal army could have fallen back to Nashville in good order, with only some of Forrest's cavalry to harass them. That, of course, would then also mean that Hood could have arrived in front of Nashville without the loss of seven thousand men and his command structure intact, and the subsequent Battle of Nashville would have been very different.

Some on the Federal side also considered the decision to withdraw to Nashville after the fight on November 30 a great blunder on the part of Schofield and Thomas, arguing that staying in place and bringing reinforcements from Nashville could have finished off Hood's army much more easily while it was on open ground and still reeling from the battle. The withdrawal instead gave Hood a two-week respite to reorganize and march to Nashville.[113]

On the Southern side, a different outcome at Spring Hill would, of course, have changed everything. Failing that, at Franklin it all revolves around Hood's decision to mount a frontal assault against the advice of all his subordinates. The Southern army's prospects change dramatically if you visualize Nathan Bedford Forrest turned loose across the river on the Federal left flank with seven thousand men and two or three hours of daylight, facing only James Wilson's cavalry, while

Hood and fifteen thousand men held the Federal mainline in place.[114] Again, the picture at Franklin and also Nashville changes drastically. In any case, however, given the condition of the Confederacy as a whole at the beginning of December 1864, it's almost impossible to see how anything Hood might have reasonably accomplished in Tennessee could have done more than prolong the agony.

Finally, it seems fitting to let the Battle of Franklin be summed up in the words of someone who was actually there and saw it all—the awesome pageantry and terrifying grandeur, the incredible valor and hopeless desperation and, ultimately, the unspeakably tragic waste as so many brave men in blue and gray fought and died in a river of blood, with no real hope of changing the ultimate outcome.

Sam Watkins grew up near Columbia, Tennessee, thirty miles or so from the battlefield, and was with the Army of Tennessee from the beginning to the end. Sam went through the locust grove with Company "H", 1st Tennessee Infantry of John C. Carter's brigade, fought the men from Illinois and Ohio in Fountain Branch Carter's garden and spent the night huddled against the outside wall of the Federal works. Eighteen years later, Watkins wrote one of the best common soldier memoirs to come out of the war, with many fine stories and a lively sense of humor, but at the beginning of his account of Franklin, he becomes deadly serious and approaches the battle this way:

> *Kind reader, my pen and courage and ability fail me…Would to God I could tear the page from these memoirs and from my own memory. It is the blackest page in the history of the war of the Lost Cause. It was the bloodiest battle of modern times…It was the finishing stroke to the independence of the Southern Confederacy. I was there. I saw it…I cannot describe it. It beggars description. Would to God I had never witnessed such a scene!*[115]

After the Battle of Franklin, the Army of Tennessee, like the Confederacy as a whole, was a mortally wounded beast, and Nashville would be its death throes. Looking back, we can search the records and try to separate the fact from the myth. We can try to draw intelligent conclusions from what we've learned, but we can never know what it was really like.

Sam Watkins knew what it was like to march day after day, half starved and half clothed, in an army that looked like it was composed of homeless people but, in fact, contained some of the bravest and most dangerous warriors on the face of the earth. Soldiers on both sides knew what was it like to watch a seemingly endless wave of men come toward you across a field, intent on taking your life, or to charge a fortified line and see all your officers killed and your friends shot to pieces all around you. Shortly, the

The Fiftieth Reunion. In 1914, these old soldiers had their photograph taken standing in front of the south wall of the Carter smokehouse. *Carter House Archives.*

survivors of the Army of Tennessee would also know what it was like to go home to a devastated country and try to put their lives back together. For the most part, the men on both sides were average folks, trying to get by in turbulent times, take care of their own and survive with a little dignity.

In some ways, the Civil War seems to belong to another time and another place far away, but when I'm walking in Fountain Branch Carter's yard, telling visitors the stories of the battle and of the men who fought and died where they're standing, as I have done many times, it seems close enough that you might almost reach out and touch it.

In case you think that the Battle of Franklin was over almost 150 years ago, as this manuscript was being prepared human remains were discovered at a construction site a few hundred yards north of Winstead Hill, General Hood's command post, and from the evidence, it is almost certainly the body of a Civil War soldier. He was rather tall for his time, buried with his boots on and wearing a long coat with Federal infantry buttons. As this book went to press, the soldier was reburied with full military honors in a local Franklin cemetery. Whether he was Federal or Confederate, a casualty of the November 30 battle or, more likely, killed in a skirmish during the retreat from Nashville two and a half weeks later, doesn't really matter. This soldier serves to remind all of us who live in a place like Franklin or near the site of any other Civil War battle that no matter how much of the twenty-first century we see around us, we still walk on dark and bloody ground.

EPILOGUE

The Commanders

FEDERAL

Abraham Lincoln

Twenty-two days before the Battle of Franklin, Abraham Lincoln was elected to a second term as president. Four and a half months later, he was assassinated by John Wilkes Booth. Lincoln did at least live to see the surrender of Lee's army at Appomattox, which effectively ended the war.

Abraham Lincoln, president of the United States. Lincoln appointed U.S. Grant general of the army on March 12, 1864. *Library of Congress.*

Ulysses S. Grant

Grant came out of the war a national hero. Elected president in 1868, for the next eight years he presided over one of the most corrupt administrations in American history. In 1881, he was financially ruined, the victim of a swindle and also learned that he had throat cancer. Ex-presidents at the time received no pension, but Grant managed to provide for his family by writing his memoirs, which he finished a few days before his death in 1885. They were published by Mark Twain and eventually earned the Grant family almost $500,000.

Lieutenant General Ulysses S. Grant. Grant approved Sherman's plan of sending George Thomas to secure Tennessee prior to beginning his "March to the Sea." *Library of Congress.*

William Tecumseh Sherman

When Sherman's old commander Grant took office as president, Sherman was made commanding general of the army. Once asked about his close relationship with Grant, the man who engaged in the brutal "March to the Sea" said, "He stood by me when I was crazy and I stood by him when he was drunk." Sherman retired in 1884 and later that year was proposed as a candidate for the presidency by the Republican Party. Having a lifelong aversion to both newspapermen and politicians, he replied, "If drafted, I will not run; if nominated, I will not accept; if elected, I will not serve." Sherman died in 1891.

Major General William Tecumseh Sherman. Sherman sent George Thomas to hold Tennessee but kept the best troops and equipment for his own campaign through Georgia. *Library of Congress.*

George Henry Thomas

A native Virginian who stayed loyal to the Union, Thomas may have been the most consistently successful, competent and dependable general officer in the Union army. He was always prepared, never squandered his men in hasty, ill-advised attacks and never lost a battle. During the war, Thomas destroyed two Confederate armies and saved at least one Federal one. Lacking the political connections of officers like Grant and Sherman, however, he spent most of the war serving under other men. Instead of writing his memoirs, as most of his contemporaries did, Thomas actually destroyed most of his private papers rather than see, as he said, "his life hawked in print for the eyes of the curious." Assigned to command the Division of the Pacific after the war, Thomas died of a stroke at the Presidio in San Francisco in 1870, age fifty-three, and was buried at Troy, New York, his wife's home. None of his relatives from Virginia came to the funeral.

Major General George Henry Thomas. Thomas was in overall command of the Union forces in Tennessee. *Library of Congress.*

John McAllister Schofield

Schofield remained in the army after the war and served for a time as secretary of war under Andrew Johnson. He later served for five years as superintendent at West Point, and from 1888 until his retirement in 1895 he was the commanding general of the army. Schofield died in 1906. In 1892, he was awarded the Medal of Honor for a Civil War action, and Schofield Barracks just outside of Honolulu is named for him.

Major General John McAllister Schofield. Schofield was in command of the Union troops who fought at Spring Hill and Franklin. *Library of Congress.*

David Sloane Stanley

Major General David Sloane Stanley, commander of the Union 4th Corps under Schofield. As senior officer on the field, Stanley conducted the defense of Spring Hill on November 29, 1864. *Library of Congress.*

At Franklin, Stanley commanded the 4th Union Corps, but the 4th Corps men who fought in the Federal mainline were temporally assigned to General Jacob Cox who actually conducted the defense. Even so, Stanley rode forward when the Confederates broke through in the center and helped to rally retreating troops. After a few minutes, Stanley was wounded near the Carter House and sent to the rear. Twenty-nine years later, Stanley was awarded the Medal of Honor for this action. After the war, Stanley remained in the army, serving in many posts in the West. He died in 1902, age seventy-three.

Jacob Dolson Cox

Brigadier General Jacob Dolson Cox. A division commander under John Schofield, Cox was temporarily given command of the Union 23rd Corps and elements of the 4th Corps at Franklin. Cox prepared the Union defenses and conducted the battle on the field. *Library of Congress.*

Because of his commander's involvement in moving his supply train over the Harpeth River, the organization and conduct of the defense at the Battle of Franklin fell to Brigadier General Cox. He held his position and inflicted over three times the casualties he suffered, and he was promoted to major general for his actions. After the war, Cox served as governor of Ohio, as well as U.S. representative and secretary of the interior. Cox later served as dean of the Cincinnati Law School and president of the University of Cincinnati. In later years, Cox wrote extensively about his wartime experiences, with his monograph on the Battle of Franklin being the best account from a Federal command perspective. Cox died in 1900.

George Day Wagner

General Wagner's failure to bring his two brigades of skirmishers inside the main works at Franklin before the Confederate attack led directly to the temporary breach of the Federal center by the divisions of Patrick Cleburne and John Brown. Wagner was swept to the rear trying to rally his fleeing men and took no further part in the battle. Nine days later, Wagner ask to be relieved and was mustered out of the army in August 1865. Wagner moved back to Indiana and died unexpectedly in February 1869.

Brigadier General George Day Wagner. In violation of his orders, Wagner left two of his brigades in front of the works at Franklin. They were overwhelmed, and their retreat led to the rupture of the center of the Union line early in the fight. *Library of Congress.*

Samuel Emerson Opdycke

Colonel Opdycke risked a court-martial for insubordination when he refused General Wagner's order to place his brigade in an exposed forward position in front of the Federal works at Franklin, but his actions placed him and his men in position to come forward and seal the break in the line at the Carter House not long afterward. For his valiant actions at Franklin, Colonel Opdycke was promoted to brigadier general. After the war, Opdycke became a businessman in New York City. In 1884, at the age of fifty-four, he died of a gunshot wound, having accidently shot himself while cleaning his pistol.

Colonel Emerson Opdycke. At Franklin, Opdycke defied his commander and led his men behind the Carter House to rest. Because of this, his brigade was in position to stop the Confederate breakthrough in the Union center about ninety minutes later. *Library of Congress.*

CONFEDERATE

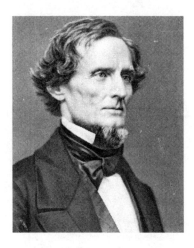

Jefferson Finis Davis, president of the Confederate States of America. Davis personally selected the senior commanders of the Army of Tennessee prior to the Tennessee Campaign. *Library of Congress.*

General Pierre Gustave Toutant Beauregard, commander of the Confederate Military Division of the West. Beauregard was John Bell Hood's immediate superior and approved his plan for the Tennessee Campaign. *Library of Congress.*

Jefferson Davis

As president of the Confederacy, Davis and his cabinet fled Richmond on April 3, 1865, and formally dissolved the government on May 5. Five days later, Davis was captured and was kept in prison at Fortress Monroe for two years. Eventually, the charges of treason against him were dropped, and Davis went back to private life. He died in New Orleans in 1889, age eighty-one. His body was carried by special train for burial in Richmond. It is said that, all along the way, the tracks were lined with mourners.

Pierre Gustave Toutant Beauregard

Born in 1818 of a prominent Creole family in Louisiana, Beauregard became one of the first general officers appointed by the Confederate States and commanded the firing of the first shot of the war on Fort Sumter. His relationship with John Bell Hood was not a happy one, and after the Tennessee Campaign debacle, Hood resigned and Beauregard went to North Carolina, where he surrendered in April 1865. After the war, Beauregard returned to Louisiana, where he was involved in the railroad business and invented a system of cable-run streetcars. Along the way, he was, at one time or another, offered command of the armies of both Romania and Egypt but declined. Beauregard died in New Orleans in 1893.

John Bell Hood

After requesting to be relieved in January 1865, Hood planned to join the troops in Texas but was unable to do so before the Confederacy collapsed. After the war, Hood moved to Louisiana and became involved in the cotton and insurance businesses. In 1868, Hood married Anna Marie Hennen and fathered eleven children in eleven years, including three sets of twins. In 1879, a yellow fever epidemic destroyed Hood's insurance business and killed him, his wife and his oldest daughter, leaving his other ten children orphans.

Lieutenant General John Bell Hood, commander of the Army of Tennessee. Hood proposed the Tennessee Campaign, planning to capture Nashville and march to the Ohio River. *Library of Congress.*

Alexander Peter Stewart

Stewart's corps was mauled at Franklin from the Harpeth River to the cotton gin. Two weeks later, it practically disintegrated in the retreat from Nashville. Following the Tennessee Campaign, Stewart fought in North Carolina under Joseph Johnston and was paroled on May 1, 1865. After the war, Stewart served as the chancellor of the University of Mississippi and the commissioner of the Chickamauga and Chattanooga National Military Park. Stewart died at Biloxi, Mississippi, in 1908, one of the last two surviving Confederate lieutenant generals.

Lieutenant General Alexander Peter Stewart, corps commander, Army of Tennessee. Stewart's three divisions attacked the Union left at Franklin. *Tennessee State Library and Archives.*

Major General Benjamin Franklin Cheatham, corps commander, Army of Tennessee. Cheatham's men attacked the center at Franklin and temporarily carried a part of the Union line as far as the Carter House. *Library of Congress.*

Benjamin Franklin Cheatham

Two of Frank Cheatham's three divisions were shattered at Franklin and his officer corps was decimated. Five of the six general officers killed at Franklin were under his command. After the Tennessee Campaign, Cheatham also went to North Carolina, where he surrendered in April 1865. After the war, Cheatham returned to Tennessee and served as superintendent of the Tennessee State Prison and postmaster of Nashville. He died in Nashville in 1886. Cheatham's son later became a major general like his father and served with distinction in the Spanish-American War and World War I.

Lieutenant General Steven Dill Lee, corps commander, Army of Tennessee. Lee's troops were the last to reach the field at Franklin, and only one of his divisions was engaged. *Library of Congress.*

Steven Dill Lee

Only one of Lee's three divisions was engaged at Franklin, and at Nashville, Lee's corps was the only one that retained its organization during the retreat into Alabama. Like Hood's other two corps commanders, Lee surrendered in North Carolina in April 1865. After the war, Lee moved to Columbus, Mississippi, where he became a planter, a state senator and the first president of what became Mississippi State University. He was also active in the United Confederate Veterans, becoming its commander in chief in 1904. Lee died at Vicksburg, Mississippi, in 1908.

Nathan Bedford Forrest

Relegated to the sidelines by his own commander, Forrest played little part at Franklin or at Nashville, being sent instead to Murfreesboro. During the retreat from Nashville, Forrest organized and commanded the rear guard, managing to keep the Federal troops at bay long enough for the rest of Hood's army to escape. Promoted to lieutenant general after the Tennessee Campaign, Forrest's cavalry was surrendered, as part of General Richard Taylor's department, on May 4, 1865. After the war, Forrest became an early member of the newly formed Ku Klux Klan but left it when its focus changed, and in his later years spoke against its violence and racism. A millionaire in prewar Memphis, Forrest was financially ruined by the war and never recovered. He spent

Major General Nathan Bedford Forrest, commander of the Confederate cavalry during the Tennessee Campaign. Hood refused Forrest's request to conduct a flanking movement at Franklin in favor of a direct assault, and his cavalry played only a minor part in the battle. *Douglas W. Bostick.*

his last years running a prison work farm on President's Island in the Mississippi River. Forrest died in October 1877.

Generally regarded as America's greatest cavalryman, Forrest's tactics and battles have been studied ever since by future generals like Erwin Rommel and George S. Patton. He once said of the war, noting that he had personally killed thirty-one Yankees in battle and had thirty horses shot from under him, "I was one horse ahead at the end." Seventy-eight years after Forrest surrendered, his great-grandson and namesake, Brigadier General Nathan Bedford Forrest III, was killed flying a B-17 over Germany.

The Carter House today. *Alan Corry photo*.

The Carter House on the 144th anniversary of the battle. Volunteers are placing almost ten thousand luminaries along the street to honor the men killed and wounded here in1864. *Preston Ryon*.

OTHERS

John and Carrie McGavock

One year after the war ended, a group of Franklin citizens raised money to have the Confederate dead moved from their original burial site in the fields south of the Carter House to a permanent resting place on land donated by John and Carrie McGavock. Eventually, 1,481 bodies were moved to a two-acre plot at Carnton known as the McGavock Confederate Cemetery. It remains today as the largest private military cemetery in the country. For the rest of her life, Carrie maintained a handwritten journal with details of every grave. John died in 1891 and Carrie followed in 1905.

The Carter House

Built in 1830 by Fountain Branch Carter, the Carter House passed to his son, Moscow, upon his father's death in 1871 and was owned by the family until 1896. In 1951, the Carter House was purchased by the State of Tennessee and was opened to the public in 1953 as a historic site. The four original buildings are said to contain over one thousand bullet holes. Today it hosts almost forty thousand visitors per year.

APPENDIX

Order of Battle

Spring Hill, Tennessee
Franklin, Tennessee
November 29–30, 1864

(Notes: compiled by David Fraley, director and historian of the Carter House; all material is from *War of the Rebellion: Official Records of the Union and Confederate Armies*, series I, volume 65, part I.)

Part I

CSA Forces

Lieutenant General John Bell Hood, Commanding

✳✳✳

Lieutenant General
Stephen Dill Lee's Corps

Aggregate Present: Lee's Corps (November 6, 1864):　　　　12,782
Effective Total Present: Lee's Corps (November 6, 1864):　　　8,632

Major General Edward Johnson's Division

Aggregate Present: Johnson's Division (November 6, 1864):　　4,029
Effective Total Present: Johnson's Division (November 6, 1864):　2,754

Brigadier General Zachariah C. Deas' Brigade

19th Alabama Infantry
22nd Alabama Infantry (Major E.H. Armistead, cmdg.—WIA)
25th Alabama Infantry
38th Alabama Infantry
50th Alabama Infantry

Brigadier General Arthur Middleton Manigault's Brigade
(Brigadier General A.M. Manigault, cmdg.—WIA)

24th Alabama Infantry (Colonel N.N. Davis, cmdg.—WIA)
28th Alabama Infantry

34th Alabama Infantry
10th South Carolina Infantry
19th South Carolina Infantry (Colonel T.P. Shaw, cmdg.—WIA)

Brigadier General Jacob H. Sharp's Brigade

7th Mississippi Infantry (Colonel W.H. Bishop, cmdg. 7th and 9th Miss. Inf.—KIA)
9th Mississippi Infantry
10th Mississippi Infantry (Colonel W.H. Sims, cmdg. 10th and 44th Miss. Inf.—WIA)
41st Mississippi Infantry (Colonel J.M. Hicks, cmdg.—WIA)
44th Mississippi Infantry
9th Mississippi Battalion Sharpshooters

Brigadier General William F. Brantley's Brigade

24th Mississippi Infantry
27th Mississippi Infantry
29th Mississippi Infantry (Major G.W. Reynolds, cmdg.—KIA)
30th Mississippi Infantry (Lieutenant Colonel J.M. Johnson, cmdg.—WIA)
34th Mississippi Infantry

MAJOR GENERAL
CARTER LITTLEPAGE STEVENSON'S DIVISION

Aggregate Present: Stevenson's Division (November 6, 1864): 4,489
Effective Total Present: Stevenson's Division (November 6, 1864): 3,039

Colonel Elihu P. Watkins's Brigade

24th Georgia Infantry
36th Georgia Infantry
39th Georgia Infantry
56th Georgia Infantry

Brigadier Edmund W. Pettus's Brigade

20th Alabama Infantry
23rd Alabama Infantry
30th Alabama Infantry
31st Alabama Infantry
46th Alabama Infantry

MAJOR GENERAL HENRY D. CLAYTON'S DIVISION

Aggregate Present: Clayton's Division (November 6, 1864):   3,247
Effective Total Present: Clayton's Division (November 6, 1864):   2,059

Brigadier General Marcellus A. Stovall's Brigade

40th Georgia Infantry
41st Georgia Infantry
42nd Georgia Infantry
43rd Georgia Infantry
52nd Georgia Infantry

Brigadier General Randall L. Gibson's Brigade

1st Louisiana Infantry
4th Louisiana Infantry
4th Louisiana Battalion
13th Louisiana Infantry
14th Louisiana Battalion Sharpshooters
16th Louisiana Infantry
19th Louisiana Infantry
20th Louisiana Infantry
25th Louisiana Infantry
30th Louisiana Infantry

Brigadier General James Holtzclaw's Brigade

18th Alabama Infantry
32nd Alabama Infantry
36th Alabama Infantry
38th Alabama Infantry
58th Alabama Infantry

Lee's Corps Artillery

Aggregate Present: Lee's Corps Artillery (November 6, 1864): 909
Effective Total Present: Lee's Corps Artillery (November 6, 1864): 705

Johnston's Battalion
Corput's Georgia Battery
Marshall's Tennessee Battery
Stephen Georgia / 3rd Maryland Battery
Courtney's Battalion
Dent's Alabama Battery
Douglas's Texas Battery
Garrity's Alabama Battery
Eldridge's Battalion
Eufaula Alabama Battery
Fenner's Louisiana Battery
Stanford's Mississippi Battery

✳✳✳

Lieutenant General
Alexander Peter Stewart's Corps

Aggregate Present: Stewart's Corps (November 6, 1864): 12,684
Effective Total Present: Stewart's Corps (November 6, 1864): 8,708

APPENDIX

Major General William Wing Loring's Division

Aggregate Present: Loring's Division (November 6, 1864):   4,959
Effective Total Present: Loring's Division (November 6, 1864):   3,575

Brigadier General Winfield Scott Featherston's Brigade

Killed: 16 Officers / 60 Men   Total Killed: 76
Wounded: 22 Officers / 178 Men   Total Wounded: 200
Missing: 4 Officers / 72 Men   Total Missing: 76
Total Casualties: 352

1st Mississippi Infantry
1st Mississippi Battalion Sharpshooters
3rd Mississippi Infantry (Colonel S.M. Dyer, cmdg.—WIA)
(3rd Mississippi Infantry's battle flag was captured)
22nd Mississippi Infantry
(22nd Mississippi Infantry's battle flag was captured)
31st Mississippi Infantry (Colonel M.D.L. Stephens, cmdg.—WIA)
33rd Mississippi Infantry
(33rd Mississippi Infantry's battle flag was captured)
40th Mississippi Infantry

Brigadier General John Adams's Brigade
(Brigadier General John Adams, cmdg.—KIA)

Killed: 10 Officers / 34 Men   Total Killed: 44
Wounded: 39 Officers / 232 Men   Total Wounded: 261
Missing: 1 Officer / 21 Men   Total Missing: 22
Total Casualties: 327

6th Mississippi Infantry
14th Mississippi Infantry
15th Mississippi Infantry (Colonel Mike Farrell, cmdg.—mortally WIA)
(15th Mississippi Infantry's battle flag was captured)
20th Mississippi Infantry (Lieutenant Colonel W.A. Rorer, cmdg.—mortally WIA)

23rd Mississippi Infantry
43rd Mississippi Infantry

Brigadier General Thomas M. Scott's Brigade
(Brigadier General Thomas M. Scott, cmdg.—WIA)

Killed: 2 Officers / 29 men   Total Killed: 31
Wounded: 23 Officers / 125 men   Total Wounded: 148
Missing: 2 Officers / 6 Men   Total Missing: 8
                                                                        Total Casualties: 187

27th Alabama Infantry (Colonel S.S. Ives, cmdg. 27th, 35th and 49th Ala.
   Inf.—WIA)
35th Alabama Infantry
49th Alabama Infantry
55th Alabama Infantry
57th Alabama Infantry (Colonel C.J.L. Cunningham, cmdg.—WIA)
12th Louisiana Infantry (Colonel Noel Ligdon Nelson, cmdg.—mortally
   WIA)

MAJOR GENERAL SAMUEL
GARRARD FRENCH'S DIVISION

Aggregate Present / French's Division (November 6, 1864):   3,090
Effective Total Present / French's Division (November 6, 1864):   1,999

Brigadier General Matthew D. Ector's Brigade
(Colonel David Coleman, cmdg.)

29th North Carolina Infantry
30th North Carolina Infantry
9th Texas Infantry
10th Texas (Dismounted) Cavalry

14th Texas (Dismounted) Cavalry
32nd Texas (Dismounted) Cavalry
[General Ector's brigade was present at Franklin, but was on detached duty and did not take part in the assault.]

Brigadier General Francis Marion Cockrell's Brigade (Brigadier General F.M. Cockrell, cmdg.—WIA November 30)

Officers Engaged: 82
Men Engaged: 614
Total Engaged: 696
Killed: 19 officers / 79 men
Wounded: 31 officers / 198 men
Missing: 13 officers / 79 men

Total Killed: 9
Total Wounded: 229
Total Missing: 92
Total Casualties: 419

1st Missouri Infantry (Colonel Hugh A. Garland, cmdg. 1st and 4th Mo. Inf.—KIA)
(1st and 4th Missouri Infantry's battle flag was captured by Corporal Peter M. Woolf, Co. A, 88th Illinois Infantry)
1st Missouri (Dismounted) Cavalry (Colonel Elijah Gates, cmdg. 1st and 3rd Mo. Cav.—WIA)
2nd Missouri Infantry (Colonel W.F. Carter, cmdg. 2nd and 6th Mo. Inf.—WIA)
(2nd and 6th Missouri Consolidated Infantry's battle flag was captured)
3rd Missouri Infantry (Captain Patrick Canniff, cmdg. 3rd and 5th Mo. Inf.—KIA)
3rd Missouri (Dismounted) Cavalry
4th Missouri Infantry
5th Missouri Infantry
6th Missouri Infantry

Brigadier General Claudius Sears's Brigade

4th Mississippi Infantry (Colonel T.N. Adaire, cmdg.—WIA)
7th Mississippi Infantry Battalion

35th Mississippi Infantry
36th Mississippi Infantry (Colonel W.W. Witherspoon, cmdg.—KIA)
39th Mississippi Infantry
46th Mississippi Infantry (Major T.D. Magee, cmdg.—WIA)

Major General
Edward Cary Walthall's Division

Aggregate Present: Walthall's Division (November 6, 1864):   3,568
Effective Total Present: Walthall's Division (November 6, 1864):   2,304

> *My command, now numbering but 1,400 guns, was the center of the corps, and presented two brigades front* [Quarles's on the right and Reynolds's on the left], *with Cantey's, under command of Brig. Gen. C.M. Shelley, in reserve.*
> *–Report of Major General E.C. Walthall regarding battle of Franklin*

Brigadier General William Andrew Quarles's Brigade
(Brigadier General W.A. Quarles, cmdg.—WIA)

1st Alabama Infantry (Major/acting Lieutenant Colonel Samuel Luckie Knox, cmdg.—mortally WIA)
(1st Alabama Infantry's battle flag was captured)
42nd Tennessee Infantry (Colonel Issac N. Hume, cmdg.—WIA)
(42nd Tennessee Infantry's battle flag was captured)
46th Tennessee Infantry (Major Sylvester C. Cooper, cmdg.—WIA and captured)
48th Tennessee Infantry
49th Tennessee Infantry (Lieutenant Colonel T.M. Atkins, cmdg.—WIA and captured)
53rd Tennessee Infantry (Captain James J. Rittenbury, cmdg.—WIA and captured)
(53rd Tennessee Infantry's battle flag was captured)
55th Tennessee Infantry (Major J.E. McDonald, cmdg.—KIA)

Brigadier General Charles M. Shelley's Brigade

17th Alabama Infantry (Colonel Virgil S. Murphey, cmdg.—WIA and captured)
26th Alabama Infantry (Colonel J.S. Garvin, cmdg.—WIA)
29th Alabama Infantry (Captain A.V. Gardner, cmdg.—WIA)
37th Mississippi Infantry

Brigadier General Daniel H. Reynolds's Brigade

1st Arkansas Mounted Rifles (Dismounted)
2nd Arkansas Mounted Rifles (Dismounted)
4th Arkansas Infantry
9th Arkansas Infantry (Major J.C. Bratton, cmdg.—WIA)
25th Arkansas Infantry

Stewart's Corps Artillery

Aggregate Present: Stewart's Corps Artillery (November 6, 1864):   958
Effective Total Present: Stewart's Corps Artillery (November 6, 1864):   760

Myrick's Battalion
Bouanchaud's Louisiana Battery
Cowan's Mississippi Battery
Darden's Mississippi Battery
Storr's Battalion
Guibor's Missouri Battery
Hoskin's Mississippi Battery
Kolb's Alabama Battery
Trueheart's Battalion
Lumsden's Alabama Battery
Selden's Alabama Battery
Tarrant's Alabama Battery

***

Major General Benjamin Franklin Cheatham's Corps

Aggregate Present: Cheatham's Corps (November 6, 1864):   15,243
Effective Total Present: Cheatham's Corps (November 6, 1864):   10,519

MAJOR GENERAL PATRICK RONAYNE CLEBURNE'S DIVISION (MAJOR GENERAL P.R. CLEBURNE, CMDG.—KIA)

Aggregate Present: Cleburne's Division (November 6, 1864):   5,742
Effective Total Present: Cleburne's Division (November 6, 1864): 3,962

Brigadier General Mark Perrin Lowrey's Brigade

16th Alabama Infantry (Colonel Frederick A. Ashford, cmdg.—KIA)
(16th Alabama Infantry's battle flag was captured by Private John H. Ricksecker, Co. D, 104th Ohio Infantry)
33rd Alabama Infantry (Colonel R.F. Crittenden, cmdg.—captured)
(33rd Alabama Infantry's battle flag was captured)
45th Alabama Infantry (Lieutenant Colonel R.H. Abercrombie, cmdg.—WIA)
(45th Alabama Infantry's battle flag was captured)
3rd Mississippi Infantry Battalion
5th Mississippi Infantry (Colonel John Weir, cmdg.—WIA)
8th Mississippi Infantry
32nd Mississippi Infantry (Colonel W.H.H. Tison, cmdg.—WIA)

Brigadier General Daniel Chevalier Govan's Brigade

3rd Confederate Infantry (PACS) (Major M.H. Dixon, cmdg.—captured)
1st Arkansas Infantry (Captain M.P. Garrett, cmdg. 1st and 15th Ark. Inf.—KIA)
2nd Arkansas Infantry (Major A.T. Meek, cmdg. 2nd and 24th Ark. Inf.—KIA)

5th Arkansas Infantry
(5th and 6th Arkansas Infantry's battle flag was captured by Corporal Benjamin Newman, Co. G, 88th Illinois Infantry)
6th Arkansas Infantry
7th Arkansas Infantry
8th Arkansas Infantry
13th Arkansas Infantry
15th Arkansas Infantry
19th Arkansas Infantry
24th Arkansas Infantry

Brigadier General Hiram Bronson Granbury's Brigade
(Brigadier General H.B. Granbury, cmdg.—KIA)

5th Confederate Infantry (PACS) (Captain A.A. Cox, cmdg.—captured)
35th Tennessee Infantry
6th Texas Infantry (Captain Rhodes Fisher, cmdg. 6th and 15th Tex. Inf.—captured)
7th Texas Infantry (Captain J.W. Brown, cmdg.—captured)
10th Texas Infantry (Lieutenant Colonel Robert Butler Young, cmdg.—KIA)
15th Texas Infantry
17th Texas (Dismounted) Cavalry
18th Texas (Dismounted) Cavalry
24th Texas (Dismounted) Cavalry (Major W.A. Taylor, cmdg. 24th and 25th Tex. Cav.—captured)
25th Texas (Dismounted) Cavalry

Brigadier James Argyle Smith's Brigade

1st Georgia Infantry
54th Georgia Infantry
57th Georgia Infantry
63rd Georgia Infantry

Major General John Calvin Brown's Division
(Major General J.C. Brown, cmdg.—WIA)

Aggregate Present: Brown's Division (November 6, 1864):   5,322
Effective Total Present: Brown's Division (November 6, 1864):   3,715

Brigadier General States Rights Gist's Brigade

(Brigadier General S.R. Gist, cmdg.—mortally WIA, died late evening, November 30)

2nd Georgia Battalion Sharpshooters
46th Georgia Infantry (Major S.J.C. Dunlap, cmdg.—WIA)
65th Georgia Infantry
16th South Carolina Infantry
24th South Carolina Infantry (Colonel Ellison Capers, cmdg.—WIA)
(Lieutenant James A. Tillman, 24th South Carolina Infantry, captured the battle flag of the 97th Ohio Infantry)

Brigadier General John C. Carter's Brigade

(Brigadier General J.C. Carter, cmdg.—mortally WIA, died December 10)

1st Tennessee Infantry
4th Tennessee Infantry (PACS)
6th Tennessee Infantry
(Private Clay Barnes, 6th Tennessee Infantry, captured the battle flag of the 44th Missouri Infantry)
8th Tennessee Infantry
9th Tennessee Infantry
16th Tennessee Infantry
28th Tennessee Infantry
50th Tennessee Infantry

Brigadier General Otho French Strahl's Brigade
(Brigadier General O.F. Strahl, cmdg.—KIA)

4th Tennessee Infantry
5th Tennessee Infantry
19th Tennessee Infantry
24th Tennessee Infantry (Colonel J.A. Wilson, cmdg.—WIA
31st Tennessee Infantry (Lieutenant Colonel F.E.P. Stafford, cmdg.—KIA)
33rd Tennessee Infantry
38th Tennessee Infantry
41st Tennessee Infantry

Brigadier General George Washington Gordon's Brigade
(Brigadier General G.W. Gordon, cmdg.—WIA and captured)

11th Tennessee Infantry
12th Tennessee Infantry
13th Tennessee Infantry
(Corporal Willey Crook, 13th Tennessee Infantry, captured the battle flag
   of the 57th Indiana Infantry)
29th Tennessee Infantry
47th Tennessee Infantry
51st Tennessee Infantry
52nd Tennessee Infantry
154th Tennessee Infantry (Colonel M. Magevney, cmdg.—WIA)

MAJOR GENERAL WILLIAM BRIMAGE
BATE'S DIVISION

Aggregate Present: Bate's Division (November 6, 1864):   5,322
Effective Total Present: Bate's Division (November 6, 1864):   2,106

*My loss in this engagement was 47 killed, 253 wounded, and 19 missing
—Report of Major General W.B. Bate regarding the Battle of Franklin*

Order of Battle

Brigadier General Thomas Benton Smith's Brigade

4th Georgia Battalion Sharpshooters
37th Georgia Infantry
2nd Tennessee Infantry
10th Tennessee Infantry
20th Tennessee Infantry
37th Tennessee Infantry

Colonel Robert Bullock's Brigade

1st Florida Infantry (Lieutenant Colonel E. Badger, cmdg. 1st and 4th Fla. Inf.—WIA)
1st Florida (Dismounted) Cavalry
3rd Florida Infantry
4th Florida Infantry
6th Florida Infantry
7th Florida Infantry

Brigadier General Henry R. Jackson's Brigade

1st Georgia Infantry (PACS) (Colonel George A. Smith, cmdg.—KIA)
1st Georgia Battalion Sharpshooters
25th Georgia Infantry
29th Georgia Infantry
30th Georgia Infantry
66th Georgia Infantry (Lieutenant Colonel A.S. Hamilton, cmdg.—WIA)

Cheatham's Corps Artillery

Aggregate Present: Cheatham's Corps Artillery (November 6, 1864): 880
Effective Total Present: Cheatham's Corps Artillery (November 6, 1864): 706

Cobb's Battalion
Ferguson's South Carolina Battery
Phillip's (Mebane's) Tennessee Battery
Slocomb's Louisiana (5th Co. Washington Artillery) Battery

Hoxton's Battalion
Perry's Florida Battery
Phelan's Alabama Battery
Turner's Mississippi Battery
Hotchkiss' Battalion
Bledsoe's Missouri Battery
Goldthwaite's Alabama Battery
Key's Arkansas Battery

Major General Nathan Bedford Forrest's Cavalry

Effective Strength: Forrest's Cavalry Corps (November 21, 1864): about 5,000

BRIGADIER GENERAL JAMES RONALD CHALMERS'S DIVISION

Colonel Edmund W. Rucker's Brigade

7th Alabama Cavalry
5th Mississippi Cavalry
7th Tennessee Cavalry
12th Tennessee Cavalry
14th Tennessee Cavalry
15th Tennessee Cavalry
Forrest's Regiment Cavalry

Colonel Jacob B. Biffle's Brigade

10th Tennessee Cavalry

Order of Battle

Brigadier General Abraham Buford's Division

Colonel Tyree H. Bell's Brigade

2nd Tennessee Cavalry
19th Tennessee Cavalry
20th Tennessee Cavalry
Nixon's Tennessee Cavalry

Colonel Edward Crossland's Brigade

3rd Kentucky Mounted Infantry
7th Kentucky Mounted Infantry
8th Kentucky Mounted Infantry
12th Kentucky Mounted Infantry
12th Kentucky Cavalry
Huey's Kentucky Battalion

Brigadier General William H. "Red" Jackson's Division

Brigadier General Frank C. Armstrong's Brigade

1st Mississippi Cavalry
2nd Mississippi Cavalry
28th Mississippi Cavalry
Ballentine's Mississippi Cavalry

Brigadier General Lawrence Sullivan Ross's Brigade

1st Texas Legion
3rd Texas Cavalry
6th Texas Cavalry
9th Texas Cavalry

Forrest's Cavalry Corps Artillery

Morton's Tennessee Battery

PART II

Federal Forces

Major General John M. Schofield, Commanding

***

4th Federal Corps
(Major General David S. Stanley, cmdg.—WIA; awarded Congressional Medal of Honor for actions at Battle of Franklin)

Present for duty in 4th Corps on November 30, 1864: 16, 111

1st DIVISION
(BRIGADIER GENERAL NATHAN KIMBALL, CMDG.)

1st Brigade
(Colonel Isaac M. Kirby, cmdg.)

21st Illinois Infantry (Captain William H. Jamison, cmdg.)
38th Illinois Infantry (Captain Andrew J. Pollard, cmdg.)
31st Indiana Infantry (Colonel John T. Smith, cmdg.)
81st Indiana Infantry (Major Edward G. Mathey, cmdg.)
90th Ohio Infantry (Lieutenant Colonel Samuel N. Yeoman, cmdg.)

2ⁿᵈ Brigade
(Brigadier General Walter C. Whittaker, cmdg.)

96th Illinois Infantry (Major George Hicks, cmdg.)
115th Illinois Infantry (Colonel Jesse H. Moore, cmdg.)
35th Indiana Infantry (Lieutenant Colonel Augustus G. Tassin, cmdg.)
21st Kentucky Infantry (Lieutenant Colonel James C. Evans, cmdg.)
23rd Kentucky Infantry (Lieutenant Colonel George W. Northrup, cmdg.)
40th Ohio Infantry [6 companies] (Lieutenant Colonel James Watson, cmdg.)
45th Ohio Infantry (Lieutenant Colonel John Humphrey, cmdg.)
51st Ohio Infantry (Lieutenant Colonel Charles H. Wood, cmdg.)

3rd Brigade
(Brigadier General William Grose, cmdg.)

75th Illinois Infantry (Colonel John E. Bennett, cmdg.)
80th Illinois Infantry (Captain James Cunningham, cmdg.)
84th Illinois Infantry (Colonel Louis H. Waters, cmdg.—severely wounded in right arm, near the shoulder)
9th Indiana Infantry (Colonel Isaac C.B. Suman, cmdg.)
30th Indiana Infantry [3 companies] (Captain Henry W. Lawton, cmdg.)
36th Indiana Infantry [1 company] (Lieutenant John P. Swisher, cmdg.)
84th Indiana Infantry (Major John Taylor, cmdg.)
77th Pennsylvania Infantry (Colonel Thomas E. Rose, cmdg.)

APPENDIX

2ᴺᴰ DIVISION
(BRIGADIER GENERAL GEORGE D. WAGNER, CMDG.)

1ˢᵗ Brigade
(Colonel Emerson Opdyke, cmdg.)

36ᵗʰ Illinois Infantry (Lieutenant Colonel Porter C. Olsen, cmdg.—KIA)
44ᵗʰ Illinois Infantry (Lieutenant Colonel John Russell, cmdg.)
73ʳᵈ Illinois Infantry (Major Thomas W. Motherspaw, cmdg.—mortally WIA, died December 18, 1864, in Nashville, Tennessee; his body was returned home for burial)
74ᵗʰ Illinois Infantry (Lieutenant Colonel George W. Smith, cmdg.)
88ᵗʰ Illinois Infantry (Lieutenant Colonel George W. Smith, cmdg.)
125ᵗʰ Ohio Infantry (Captain Edward Bates, cmdg.)
24ᵗʰ Wisconsin Infantry (Major Arthur MacArthur Jr., cmdg.—severely WIA)

2ⁿᵈ Brigade
(Colonel John Q. Lane, cmdg.)

100ᵗʰ Illinois Infantry (Lieutenant Colonel Charles M. Hammond, cmdg.)
40ᵗʰ Indiana Infantry (Lieutenant Colonel Henry Leaming, cmdg.)
57ᵗʰ Indiana Infantry (Major John S. McGraw, cmdg.)
28ᵗʰ Kentucky Infantry (Lieutenant Colonel J. Rowan Boone, cmdg.)
26ᵗʰ Ohio Infantry (Captain William Clark, cmdg.)
97ᵗʰ Ohio Infantry (Lieutenant Colonel Milton Barnes, cmdg.)

3ʳᵈ Brigade, Brigadier General Luther Bradley
(Colonel Joseph Conrad [Franklin], cmdg)

27ᵗʰ Illinois Infantry [6 companies] (Captain W.B. Young, cmdg.—mortally WIA)
42ⁿᵈ Illinois Infantry (Major Frederick Atwater, cmdg.)

51st Illinois Infantry (Captain Merritt B. Atwater, cmdg.)
79th Illinois Infantry (Colonel Allen Buckner, cmdg.)
15th Missouri Infantry (Captain George Ernst, cmdg.)
64th Ohio Infantry (Lieutenant Colonel Robert C. Brown, cmdg.)
65th Ohio Infantry (Major Orlow Smith, cmdg.—WIA at Spring Hill; Captain Andrew Howenstine, cmdg.—severely WIA and captured at Spring Hill; Major Coulter, of the 64th Ohio Infantry, assumed command)

3RD DIVISION
(BRIGADIER GENERAL THOMAS J. WOOD, CMDG.)

1st Brigade
(Colonel Abel D. Streight, cmdg.)

89th Illinois Infantry (Lieutenant Colonel William D. Williams, cmdg.)
51st Indiana Infantry (Captain William W. Scearce, cmdg.)
8th Kansas Infantry (Lieutenant Colonel John Conover, cmdg.)
15th Ohio Infantry (Colonel Frank Askew, cmdg.)
49th Ohio Infantry (Major Luther M. Strong, cmdg.)

2nd Brigade
(Colonel Sidney Post, cmdg.)

59th Illinois Infantry (Major James M. Stookey, cmdg.)
41st Ohio Infantry (Lieutenant Colonel Robert L. Kimberly, cmdg.)
71st Ohio Infantry (Colonel Henry K. McConnell, cmdg.)
93rd Ohio Infantry (Lieutenant Colonel Daniel Bowman, cmdg.)
124th Ohio Infantry (Lieutenant Colonel James Pickands, cmdg.)

3rd Brigade
(Colonel Frederick Knefler, cmdg.)

79th Indiana Infantry (Lieutenant Colonel George Parker, cmdg.)
86th Indiana Infantry (Colonel George F. Dick, cmdg.)
10th Kansas Infantry
17th Kentucky Infantry (Lieutenant Colonel Alexander M. Stout, cmdg.)
13th Ohio Infantry (Major Joseph T. Snider, cmdg.)
19th Ohio Infantry (Lieutenant Colonel Henry G. Stratton, cmdg.)

4th Corps Artillery

25th Indiana Light Battery (Sturm's)
1st Kentucky Battery (Captain Theodore Thomason, cmdg.—WIA)
1st Michigan Battery (De Vries)
1st Ohio Battery "G" (Captain Alexander Marshall, cmdg.)
6th Ohio Battery (Lieutenant Aaron P. Baldwin, cmdg.)
2nd Pennsylvania Battery (Captain Jacob Ziegler, cmdg.)
4th U.S. Regular Battery "M" (Lieutenant Samuel Canby, cmdg.)

***

23rd Federal Corps
Major General John M. Schofield, cmdg.
(Brigadier General Jacob Dolson Cox, in temporary command November 30, 1864)

Present for duty in 23rd Corps, November 30, 1864:   10,527

2ᴺᴰ DIVISION
(BRIGADIER GENERAL THOMAS H. RUGER, CMDG.)

1ˢᵗ Brigade
(Brigadier General Joseph A. Cooper, cmdg.)

130th Indiana Infantry (Colonel Charles S. Parrish, cmdg.)
25th Michigan Infantry (Lieutenant Colonel Benjamin F. Orent, cmdg.)
99th Ohio Infantry (Lieutenant Colonel John E. Cummins, cmdg.)
3rd Tennessee Infantry (Colonel William Cross, cmdg.)
6th Tennessee Infantry (Lieutenant Colonel Edward Maynard, cmdg.)
[General Cooper's brigade was assigned to Ruger's division but was on detached duty and not present at Franklin.]

2ⁿᵈ Brigade
(Colonel Orlando Moore, cmdg.)

107th Illinois Infantry (Colonel Francis H. Lowry, cmdg. (mortally WIA; died January 1, 1865)
80th Indiana Infantry (Lieutenant Colonel Alfred D. Owen, cmdg.)
129th Indiana Infantry (Colonel Charles A. Zollinger, cmdg.)
23rd Michigan Infantry (Colonel Oliver L. Spaulding, cmdg.)
24th Missouri Infantry
111th Ohio Infantry (Lieutenant Colonel Isaac Ruth Sherwood, cmdg.—WIA)
118th Ohio Infantry (Major Edgar Sowers, cmdg.)

3ʳᵈ Brigade
(Colonel Silas Strickland, cmdg.)

91st Indiana Infantry (Colonel John Mehringer, cmdg.)
123rd Indiana Infantry (Colonel John C. McQuiston, cmdg.)
72nd Illinois Infantry (Captain James A. Sexton, cmdg.)

44th Missouri Infantry (Colonel R.C. Bradshaw, cmdg.—severely WIA)
50th Ohio Infantry (Lieutenant Colonel Hamilton S. Gillespie, cmdg.)
183rd Ohio Infantry (Lieutenant Colonel Mervin Clark, cmdg.—KIA)

23rd Corps, Second Division Artillery

13th Indiana Battery (Harvey's)
19th Ohio Battery (Wilson's)

3RD DIVISION
(BRIGADIER GENERAL JACOB D. COX, CMDG.)

(BRIGADIER GENERAL JAMES A. REILLY, IN TEMPORARY COMMAND NOVEMBER 30, 1864)

1st Brigade
(Brigadier General James A. Reilly, cmdg.)

12th Kentucky Infantry (Lieutenant Colonel Lawrence H. Rousseau, cmdg.)
16th Kentucky Infantry (Lieutenant Colonel John S. White, cmdg.)
100th Ohio Infantry (Lieutenant Colonel Edwin L. Hayes, cmdg.)
104th Ohio Infantry (Colonel Oscar W. Sterl, cmdg.)
175th Ohio Infantry (Lieutenant Colonel Dan McCoy, cmdg.)
8th Tennessee Infantry (Captain J.W. Berry, cmdg.)

2nd Brigade
(Colonel John S. Casement, cmdg.)

65th Illinois Infantry (Lieutenant Colonel W. Scott Stewart, cmdg.)
65th Indiana Infantry (Lieutenant Colonel John W. Hammond, cmdg.)
124th Indiana Infantry
103rd Ohio Infantry
5th Tennessee Infantry (Major David G. Bowers, cmdg.)

3rd Brigade
(Colonel Israel N. Stiles, cmdg.)

112th Illinois Infantry (Lieutenant Colonel Emery S. Bond, cmdg.)
63rd Indiana Infantry (Lieutenant Colonel Daniel Morris, cmdg.)
120th Indiana Infantry (Colonel Allen W. Prather, cmdg.)
128th Indiana Infantry (Lieutenant Colonel Jasper Packard, cmdg.)

23rd Corps, Third Division Artillery

23rd Indiana Battery (Lieutenant Aaron A. Wilber, cmdg.)
1st Ohio Battery "D" (Captain Giles J. Cockerill, cmdg.)

Major General James H. Wilson's Federal Cavalry Corps

Estimated Strength: Federal cavalry at Franklin: 5,500

1ST DIVISION
(BRIGADIER GENERAL EDWARD M. McCOOK, CMDG.)

1st Brigade
(Brigadier General John T. Croxton, cmdg.)

8th Iowa Cavalry (Colonel Joseph B. Dorr, cmdg.)
4th Kentucky Mounted Infantry (Colonel Robert M. Kelly, cmdg.)
2nd Michigan Cavalry (Lieutenant Colonel Benjamin Smith, cmdg.)
1st Tennessee Cavalry (Lieutenant Colonel Calvin M. Dyer, cmdg.)

1st Division Artillery

Chicago Board of Trade Battery (Robinson's)

5TH DIVISION
(BRIGADIER GENERAL EDWARD HATCH, CMDG.)

1st Brigade
(Colonel Robert R. Stewart, cmdg.)

3rd Illinois Cavalry (Lieutenant Colonel Robert H. Carnahan, cmdg.)
11th Indiana Cavalry (Lieutenant Colonel Abram Sharra, cmdg.)
12th Missouri Cavalry (Lieutenant Colonel Robert H. Brown, cmdg.)
10th Tennessee Cavalry (Major William P. Story, cmdg.)

2nd Brigade
(Colonel Datus Coon, cmdg.)

6th Illinois Cavalry (Lieutenant Colonel John Lynch, cmdg.)
7th Illinois Cavalry (Major John M. Graham, cmdg.)

9th Illinois Cavalry (Captain Joseph W. Harper, cmdg.)
2nd Iowa Cavalry (Major Charles C. Horton, cmdg.)
12th Tennessee Cavalry (Colonel George Spaulding, cmdg.)

5th Division Artillery

1st Illinois Battery "I" (McCartney's)

6TH DIVISION
(BRIGADIER GENERAL RICHARD W. JOHNSON, CMDG.)

1st Brigade
(Colonel Thomas J. Harrison, cmdg.)

16th Illinois Cavalry (Major Charles H. Beeres, cmdg.)
5th Iowa Cavalry (Major J. Morris Young, cmdg.)
7th Ohio Cavalry (Colonel Israel Garrard, cmdg.)

2nd Brigade
(Colonel James Biddle, cmdg.)

14th Illinois Cavalry (Major Francis M. Davidson, cmdg.)
6th Indiana Cavalry (Major Jacob S. Stephens, cmdg.)
8th Michigan Cavalry (Lieutenant Colonel Grover S. Wormer, cmdg.)

6th Division Artillery

4th U.S. Regular Battery "I"

7TH DIVISION
(BRIGADIER GENERAL JOSEPH F. KNIPE, CMDG.)

1st Brigade
(Brevet Brigadier General John H. Hammond, cmdg.)

9th Indiana Cavalry (Colonel George W. Jackson, cmdg.)
10th Indiana Cavalry (Colonel Thomas N. Pace, cmdg.)
19th Pennsylvania Cavalry (Lieutenant Colonel Joseph C. Hess, cmdg.)
2nd Tennessee Cavalry (Lieutenant Colonel William F. Prosser, cmdg.)
4th Tennessee Cavalry (Major Meshack Stephens, cmdg.)

2nd Brigade
(Colonel Gilbert M.L. Johnson, dismounted, cmdg.)

12th Indiana Cavalry
13th Indiana Cavalry
8th Tennessee Cavalry

7^h Division Artillery

14th Ohio Battery (Myers's)

NOTES

Prologue

1. The army passing Carter's front door was actually commanded by Major General John McAllister Schofield. General Schofield, however, was one mile or so north, conferring with his engineering staff and trying to solve the problem of getting his eight hundred wagons and troops across the Harpeth River. He had placed Brigadier General Cox, his senior division commander, in temporary command of both divisions of the 23rd Corps plus some other units from Major General David Stanley's 4th Corps, with orders to prepare a defense of the town and the river crossing. It was in this capacity that General Cox took Mr. Carter's house as his field command post.
2. At the time of the meeting, Major Cheairs was sitting in Camp Chase, a Federal POW camp in Columbus, Ohio.
3. John Bell Hood, *Advance and Retreat* (Secaucus, NJ: Blue and Gray Press, 1985), 290.
4. Adam J. Weaver, 104th Ohio Infantry, from the Carter House Archives.

Chapter 1

5. The basic information about the background of both Lincoln and Davis is available from many sources, including the online encyclopedia Wikipedia. The information here on Davis's background, including the text of the telegram he received and much more, is from Shelby Foote, *The Civil War: A Narrative*, vol. 1 (New York, Random House, 1958), 1–17.

6. Different statistics can no doubt be found relating to the losses of the Army of Tennessee in men and material during the Atlanta Campaign for the reasons given in the text, but these are probably as accurate as any. They are from Thomas L. Connelly, *Autumn of Glory: The Army of Tennessee 1862–1865* (Baton Rouge: Louisiana State University Press, 2001) 389–90, 467–68.

7. Connelly, *Autum of Glory*, 477–81. The details of Davis's visit, the plan of action for the army and Davis's decisions on personnel changes are from Connelly above. The opinions as to some of the causes of the problems and confusion within the command structure are mine.

8. Shelby Foote, *The Civil War: A Narrative*, vol. 3 (New York: Random House, 1974), 609.

CHAPTER 2

9. John Bell Hood as quoted in Foote, *The Civil War*, vol. 3, 604.

10. Foote, *The Civil War*, vol. 3, 599.

11. Jack Hurst, *Nathan Bedford Forrest: A Biography* (New York: Alfred A. Knopf, 1993), 223; Foote, *The Civil War*, vol. 3, 600.

12. Hurst, *Nathan Bedford Forrest*, 129–30. On June 13, 1863, Forrest was shot at Columbia, Tennessee, by Lieutenant A.W. Gould, whom Forrest had ordered transferred from his command. Gould took this as a reflection on his courage, drew a pistol and shot Forrest in the left side. Forrest then deflected the pistol and fatally stabbed the young officer with his penknife. Twelve days later, Forrest was back in the saddle.

13. Benson Bobrick, *Master of War* (New York: Simon & Schuster, 2009), 39.

14. In one of the war's many curious twists, Grant, who was now their supreme commander, had been a lowly plebe (first-year man) at West Point the year Sherman and Thomas were first classmen (seniors).

15. The account of the Army of Tennessee's three-week campaign against General Sherman's supply line north from Atlanta is taken from two sources previously cited: Foote's superb *The Civil War*, vol. 3, and Thomas L. Connelly's benchmark study of the Army of Tennessee, *Autumn of Glory*.

CHAPTER 3

16. William T. Sherman, after chasing John Bell Hood for three weeks in northern Georgia. From Foote, *The Civil War*, vol. 3, 613.

17. Phil Stephenson, Washington artillery, as quoted in Sam Davis Elliott, *Soldier of Tennessee* (Baton Rouge: Louisiana State University Press, 1999), 223.

18. Aristide Hopkins, as quoted in Elliott, *Soldier of Tennessee*, 223.

19. Jacob D. Cox, *Recollection of the Civil War*, vol. 2 (N.p: Leonaur Ltd., 2007), 264–65.

20. Eric A. Jacobson, *For Cause & for Country* (Franklin, TN: O'More Publishing, 2007), 50.

21. Foote, *The Civil War*, vol. 3, 612–13.

22. Cox, *Recollections of the Civil War*, vol. 2, 269.

23. Jacobson, *For Cause & for Country*, 43, n12 and n44.

24. Ridley Walls II, *Old Enough to Die* (Franklin, TN: Hillsboro Press, 1996), 139; Letter written by Jas. L. Cooper, November 18, 1864.

25. Jacobson, *For Cause & for Country*, 48.

26. Cox, *Reflections of the Civil War*, vol. 2, 270; Jacobson, *For Cause & for Country*, 50–51.

27. Jacobson, *For Cause & for Country*, 46; Wiley Sword, *The Confederacy's Last Hurrah* (Lawrence: University of Kansas Press, n.d., reprint of 1992 original), 66–69.

28. The Battle of Johnsonville information is from Foote, *The Civil War*, vol. 3, 619–20; Hurst, *Nathan Bedford Forrest*, 226–28.

29. Hurst, *Nathan Bedford Forrest*, 230–31.

Chapter 4

30. The chapter title is from Sumner A. Cunningham, *Reminiscences of the 41st Tennessee*, edited by John A Simpson (Shippensburg, PA: White Mane Books, 2001), 93; homemade sign seen by Confederate soldiers of Cheatham's corps as they crossed the state line into Tennessee south of Waynesboro; the epigraph quote is from Connelly, *Autumn of Glory*, 492.

31. As always, opinions as to troop strength may vary widely. These numbers represent the research of David Fraley, historian of the Carter House, Franklin, Tennessee. See also Jacobson, *For Cause & for Country*, 425–26.

32. Christopher Losson, *Tennessee's Forgotten Warriors: Frank Cheatham and His Confederate Division* (Knoxville, University of Tennessee Press, 1989), 202.

33. Jacobson, *For Cause & for Country*, 55–58. The order of battle and order of march of the Confederate and Federal armies is available from several sources.

34. Cox, *Recollections of the Civil War*, 283–84.

35. Jacobson, *For Cause & for Country*, 71–75.

36. Cox, *The Battle of Franklin* (Dayton, OH: Morningside Bookshop, reprint 1983), 25, n2–n30. Thomas had, in fact, already sent a dispatch telling Schofield to withdraw to Franklin, but according to Hood's later reports, it was intercepted by the Confederates and Schofield never saw it. On the twenty-seventh, the telegraph operator at Schofield's headquarters became frightened and fell back to Franklin, where he decoded the telegraph traffic and sent it on by courier the last twenty

miles to Columbia. This was how the Confederates managed to intercept Thomas's order to Schofield telling him to fall back to Franklin—not by taping the wire but by capturing the dispatch rider.

37. Cox, *Battle of Franklin*, 27.

38. In general, the facts surrounding the action in and around Spring Hill, Tennessee, on November 29, 1864, are not in serious dispute. The exact orders given, the reasons for the actions or inaction of several of the commanders on the Confederate side and the blame for what transpired, however, continues to be the subject of debate into the twenty-first century. My brief account comes from the following sources: Sword, *Confederacy's Last Hurrah*, 111–39; Jacobson, *For Cause & for Country*, 85–183; Connelly, *Autumn of Glory*, 494–502; Thomas Jordan and J.P. Pryor, *The Campaigns of General Nathan Bedford Forrest* (N.p.: Da Capo Press, 1996), 620–25; Alethea D. Sayers, "The Last Campaign," found in Mauriel Phillips Joslyn, ed., *A Meteor Shining Brightly* (Milledgeville, GA: Terrell House Publishing, 1998), 233–61.

CHAPTER 5

39. Sword, *Confederacy's Last Hurrah*, 152. General Bradley went on to say that "[i]f only the enemy had shown his usual boldness, I think he would have beaten us disastrously."

40. Sword, *Confederacy's Last Hurrah*, 153–54. The Federal soldiers on Brown's right flank were actually a single small regiment and two additional companies from John Lane's brigade—maybe three hundred men in all—but, from a distance in the twilight, they may have looked like more of a threat than they really were. Whatever their size, historian Eric Jacobson correctly observes that they brought Brown's entire division to a halt without firing a shot.

41. Foote, *The Civil War*, vol. 3, 661.

42. A detailed account of everything that happened at Spring Hill, and an in-depth analysis of its causes and implications, is beyond the scope of this work. For anyone interested in further study, the author strongly recommends Eric A. Jacobson's recent benchmark work on the campaign, *For Cause & for Country*, pages 76 through 183.

CHAPTER 6

43. Jacobson, *For Cause & for Country*, 192. Brown also told Major Vaulx, of Frank Cheatham's staff, that Hood was angry about the Yankees getting away and that "he is going to charge the blame of it off on somebody." It soon became clear that "somebody" included both Cheatham and Pat Cleburne.

44. Jacobson, *For Cause & for Country*, 153. In this passage, Jacobson quotes General William Bate as saying, on the night of the twenty-ninth, that Hood believed that Forrest had blocked the pike north of town and that he expected the Yankees not only to be there the next morning but also to surrender without a fight.

45. Jacobson, *For Cause & for Country*, 191, n14.

46. Jordan and Pryor, *The Campaigns of General Nathan Bedford Forrest*, 624–25.

47. Hurst, *Nathan Bedford Forrest*, 233–34. Hurst goes on to speculate that, by relegating Forrest to the fringes of such a bloody battle, Hood may have saved Forrest's life.

48. Losson, *Tennessee's Forgotten Warriors*, 218.

49. Foote, *The Civil War*, vol, 3, 666.

50. Jacobson, *For Cause & for Country*, 241–42.

CHAPTER 7

51. Foote, *The Civil War*, vol., 3, 665.

52. For much of the details of the fight at Franklin, I've relied on the work of several excellent historians and participants in the battle who have been cited several times before. The opinions as to Hoods reasons for ordering the attack at Franklin, however, are mine alone.

53. Cox, *Battle of Franklin*, 39. Cox later says that General Schofield told him some years after the war that the pontoons did actually arrive by rail car before noon but were too late to be of use, since his engineers had already succeeded in putting the County Bridge back in service, from Cox, 50, n2.

54. Levi T. Scofield, *The Retreat From Pulaski to Nashville, Tennessee* (Franklin, TN: Mint Julep Printing Co., 1996, reprint), 24. This brigade was actually commanded by Colonel Thomas J. Henderson, but because he was ill that day, he turned the brigade over to Colonel Stiles, commander of the 63rd Indiana. Because of the critical situation, however, Colonel Henderson would not leave the field and stayed with his men throughout the battle, although Stiles remained in command.

55. Cox's encounter with Schofield and his assignment to conduct the defense of Franklin is from Cox, *Battle of Franklin*, 39; placement of units is from Jacobson, *For Cause & for Country*, 291, 311. Distances measured from Google Earth.

56. Captain Leander S. McGraw, 107th Illinois, as quoted in Jacobson, *For Cause & for Country*, 365.

57. Scofield, *Retreat From Pulaski*, 40.

58. Even here, there were fence posts and rails driven into the ground as an abatis, but it was still the most unobstructed approach.

59. Carter House Archives.

CHAPTER 8

60. All of the Confederate divisions in the initial attack were made up of three brigades except John C. Brown's, which had four. Samuel French's division had three brigades, but only two were present, the third being off guarding the supply train, for a total of eighteen brigades.

61. Cox, *Battle of Franklin*, 92–93.

62. Jacobson, *For Cause & for Country*, 248–49.

63. Joslyn, *A Meteor Shining Brightly*, essay by Thomas Y. Cartwright, 266–67.

64. Losson, *Tennessee's Forgotten Warriors*, 219.

65. This was the brigade commanded at Spring Hill by Luther Bradley until he was wounded. Conrad had been in command for less than twenty-four hours.

66. The story of Opdycke's insubordination is from Jacobson, *For Cause & for Country*, 230. George Wagner didn't know it, but in his frustration, he had just made his best and most important decision of the war.

67. Cox, *Battle of Franklin*, 71.

68. Scofield, *Retreat from Pulaski*, 33.

69. Ibid., 34.

70. David R. Logsdon, *Eyewitness to the Battle of Franklin* (Nashville, TN: Kettle Mills Press, 1996), 14.

CHAPTER 9

71. Letter from First Lieutenant James S. Pressnall, 63rd Indiana, Carter House Archives.

72. D.H. Patterson, quoted in *The Confederate Veteran* (March 1901): 117.

73. These Indiana and Illinois troops were armed with Henry and Spencer repeating rifles. Just these two companies could have easily fired three thousand rounds in the first sixty to ninety seconds. An equal number of men with the standard rifled musket, carried by Confederates and Federals alike, would do well to fire four to five hundred rounds in the same time.

74. Jacobson, *For Cause & for Country*, 296–97; Sword, *Confederacy's Last Hurrah*, 228.

75. General Samuel G. French, *Two Wars* (Huntington, WV: Blue Acorn Press, 1999, reprint), 296–97.

76. This version of John Adam's death follows most closely the one found in Jacobson, *For Cause & for Country*, 342–43. Other versions are found in Sword, *Confederacy's Last Hurrah*, 226–27; Cox, *Battle of Franklin*, 127–28. For a complete discussion of the various versions of Adams's death, see Jacobson above, pages 342–48.

Chapter 10

77. Joslyn, *A Meteor Shining Brightly*, essay by Thomas Y. Cartwright, 276. Cartwright quotes Captain Samuel Foster, 24th Texas Cavalry.

78. George W. Gordon as quoted in *The Confederate Veteran* (January 1900): 7.

79. James Barr, Co. E, 65th Illinois Volunteers, quoted in *Southern Bivouac* (October, 1885); the Carter House archives.

80. Jacobson, *For Cause & for Country*, 318.

81. Logsdon, *Eyewitness to the Battle of Franklin*, 12, quoting Alice Nichol, age eight.

82. Major Thomas C. Thoburn, 50th Ohio, Carter House Archives.

83. William Mohrman, 72nd Illinois, Carter House Archives.

84. Sam R. Watkins, *Company "Aytch"*, edited by Ruth Hill Fulton McAllister (Franklin, TN: Providence House Publishers, 2007), 262.

85. W.H. Newlin, *History of the 73rd Illinois Volunteer Infantry—1862–1865*, 462, courtesy of the Carter House Archives.

86. Walter B. Cisco, *States Right Gist* (Gretna, LA: Pelican Publishing Co., 2008), 140–41.

87. Statistics and estimates from Jacobson, *For Cause & for Country*, 416.

88. Jacobson, *For Cause & for Country*, 377–78; Losson, *Tennessee's Forgotten Warriors*, 226.

89. James S. Pressnall, from an undated memoir courtesy of Kathryn Crawford, Pressnall's great-great-granddaughter.

90. General Cox, in fact, sent word to General Schofield stating that he was quite willing to stay where he was and continue to hold the line. Cox wanted to have reinforcements sent down from Nashville so they could finish the job there at Franklin but was told to withdraw across the river. Cox, *Battle of Franklin*, 169, 170.

91. For a complete account of the Federal withdrawal, see Cox, *Battle of Franklin*, 186–93.

92. Jacobson, *For Cause & for Country*, 392.

Chapter 11

93. Logsdon, *Eyewitness to the Battle of Franklin*, 58.

94. Colonel Issac Sherwood, Carter House Archives.

95. Pressnall, undated manuscript.

96. Carter House Archives.

97. John McQuaide, *Confederate Veteran* (June 1899): 272; Jacobson, *For Cause & for Country*, 411–12.

98. Losson, *Tennessee's Forgotten Warriors*, 227.

99. Jacobson, *For Cause & for Country*, 408–9.

100. Logsdon, *Eyewitnesses at the Battle of Franklin*, 72.

101. Ibid., 70.

102. Jacobson, *For Cause & for Country*, 415.

103. Logsdon, *Eyewitnesses at the Battle of Franklin*, 73.

104. Ives and Bell quotes from the Carter House Archives.

105. Logsdon, *Eyewitnesses to the Battle of Franklin*, 10, 11, 71, 72.

106. Jacobson, *For Cause & for Country*, 409.

107. Lieutenant Colonel Moscow B. Carter letter, 1882, Carter House Archives.

108. Hardin Figuers manuscript, courtesy of the Carter House Archives.

Chapter 12

109. Cox, *Battle of Franklin*, 211, 215. These are the official figures. Cox states that his own investigation on the field at this time put the Confederate killed at 1,800. In all probability, even that figure is too low. Add to this the number of missing men and those wounded who had already left Franklin, and the total Confederate loss could easily have been 7,000 men or more.

110. Paul H. Stockdale, *The Death of an Army* (Murfreesboro, TN: Southern Heritage Press, 1992), 162.

111. Jacobson, *For Cause & for Country*, 428.

112. J.A. Sexton, 72nd Illinois, Carter House Archives.

113. Scofield, *Retreat From Pulaski*, 56.

114. I'm assuming that Forrest would have had most of his cavalry and William Loring's division, which would have been the nearest to the Harpeth River ford and therefore the most logical infantry force for Forrest to use.

115. Watkins, *Company "Aytch"*, 260. The words are all Sam's, but I have slightly rearranged the sentence order.

ABOUT THE AUTHOR

James R. Knight is a graduate of Harding University, 1967. He spent five years as a pilot in the United States Air Force and thirty-one years as a pilot for Federal Express, the last twenty years as a DC-10 captain. In the early '90s, he began researching a historical incident in his hometown and wrote an article that was published in the *Arkansas Historical Quarterly*. In 2003, Eakin Press published his biography of Bonnie and Clyde titled *Bonnie and Clyde: A 21st Century Update*. In 2007, he published the story and correspondence of a Confederate cavalryman titled *Letters to Anna*.

Photograph by Judy Knight.

He retired from Federal Express in 2004 and lives in Franklin, Tennessee, where he works part time as a guide at the Carter House, a local Civil War historic site. He and his wife Judy have three children and six grandchildren.

Visit us at
www.historypress.net